Being Muslim
Haroon Siddiqui

Groundwood Books
House of Anansi Press

Toronto Berkeley

Groundwood Books / House of Anansi Press
110 Spadina Avenue, Suite 801, Toronto, Ontario M5V 2K4
Distributed in the USA by Publishers Group West
1700 Fourth Street, Berkeley, CA 94710

ONTARIO ARTS COUNCIL
CONSEIL DES ARTS DE L'ONTARIO

We acknowledge for their financial support of our publishing program the Canada Council for the Arts, the Government of Canada through the Book Publishing Industry Development Program (BPIDP) and the Ontario Arts Council. Special thanks to the Ontario Media Development Corporation.

Library and Archives Canada Cataloging in Publication
Siddiqui, Haroon
Being Muslim / by Haroon Siddiqui.
(Groundwork Guides)
Includes bibliographical references and index.
ISBN-13: 978-0-88899-785-2 (bound)
ISBN-13: 978-0-88899-786-9 (pbk.)
ISBN-10: 0-88899-785-X (bound)
ISBN-10: 0-88899-786-8 (pbk.)
1. Isalm. 2. Muslims. 3. Muslims–Canada. I. Title.
II. Series.
BP161.3.S53 2006   297   C2005-907539-2

Printed and bound in Canada

GROUNDWORK GUIDES ⁴⁴⁰

Empire
James Laxer
Being Muslim
Haroon Siddiqui
Genocide
Jane Springer
Climate Change
Shelley Tanaka

Series Editor
Jane Springer

GROUNDWORK GUIDES

For my parents, the late Hafiz Mohammed Moosa Kandhlawi and the late Hafiza Amtul Baseer, for their endless love and indulgences that gave me the confidence to go anywhere, try anything.

My uncle, the late Hafiz Syed Sarwar Hussain, my first teacher and mentor, whose values continue to guide me.

My siblings, Maryam, Suleman and Hafiz Yousuf, for their enduring affection.

My wife, Yasmeen, whose animating presence lights up our household and whose judgment often saves me from mine.

Our sons, Fahad and Faisal, for whom and whose generation this book was written.

Contents

Acknowledgments

At Groundwood Books, Patsy Aldana, for asking me to write the book; and Jane Springer, Shelley Tanaka, Nan Froman and Sarah Quinn, for editing it.

My niece, Yasmeen Siddiqui, a teacher, for the research and the fact-checking; and sons, Fahad and Faisal, for help in writing the portions on politics and popular culture respectively.

My informal focus group — Peter Carpenter, Jill Goodreaugh, Lauren Larsen and Sher Singh — for feedback through various stages of writing.

Islamic scholar Zahid Abu Ghudda of Toronto, for guiding me through the religious references.

Canadian historian Desmond Morton of McGill University and *Toronto Star* columnist Carol Goar, for wading through the manuscript and straightening me out on several points.

At the *Toronto Star*, my immediate bosses for the last fifteen years, Publisher-Editor John Honderich until 2004 and Publisher Michael Goldbloom and Editor Giles Gherson since, for letting me write freely; colleague Linda Larsen, for her endless considerations; and the many editors I have worked for at the paper since 1978, for providing me unparalleled opportunities to travel the world, cover the big stories and meet some of the most influential newsmakers of the age. Some of the ideas and interviews in this book first appeared in the *Star*.

Muslims by Region / Language*

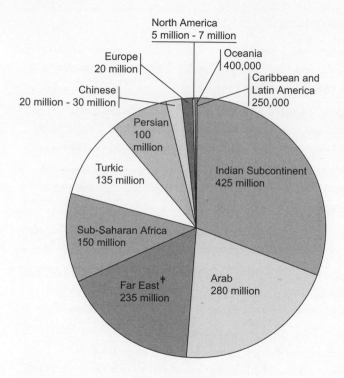

North America
5 million - 7 million

Europe
20 million

Oceania
400,000

Chinese
20 million - 30 million

Caribbean and
Latin America
250,000

Persian
100
million

Turkic
135 million

Indian Subcontinent
425 million

Sub-Saharan Africa
150 million

Far East ‡
235 million

Arab
280 million

*The total Muslim population is said to range between 1.3 and 1.6 billion. The uncertainty emanates mostly from three factors: outdated census in many nations, especially those embroiled in conflicts, such as Afghanistan, Iraq and Sudan; countries such as the US and France not recording their citizens' religion; and Muslims in some countries, such as China, hiding their identity for fear of persecution. I have relied on estimates as listed in *The World Factbook*, www.cia.gov/cia/publications/factbook/index.html.
‡The Far East includes Indonesia, Malaysia, Brunei, Singapore and adjacent areas.

Chapter 1
The Politics

UNDER SIEGE

Contrary to the popular belief that the West is under siege from Muslim terrorists, it is Muslims who have become the biggest victims of the attacks of September 11, 2001, as inconceivable as that would have seemed in the aftermath of the murder of 2,900 Americans. Since then, between 34,000 and 100,000 Iraqis have been killed by the Americans or the insurgents.[1] Nobody knows how many have been killed in Afghanistan. In the spots hit by terrorists — from London and Madrid to Amman, Istanbul, Riyadh and Jeddah, through Karachi to Bali and Jakarta — more Muslims have been killed and injured than non-Muslims.

The approximately 27 million Muslims living in Western nations have been targeted in other ways. They have been victims of racial profiling and frequent identity mix-ups at airports and border crossings, where they may be harassed and sometimes detained. Monitored by both the secret services and the media, they must be careful about what they say in emails, phone conversations and in public. They must think twice about keeping a beard or wearing overtly Muslim clothing and be mindful of their behavior in public. They must keep proving, in school and at work, that neither they nor their faith fit the caricature of Muslims and Islam drilled into the public consciousness.

They feel under siege, living through what the Canadian Arab

Federation has called "psychological internment," referring to the internment of thousands of Japanese Americans and Japanese Canadians during the Second World War. For American Muslims, the post-9/11 period has parallels with the infamous McCarthy era of the 1950s, when Senator Joseph McCarthy led a witch-hunt of suspected Communists and ruined the reputation and lives of many innocent Americans.

Muslims, therefore, have reasons to be angry at George W. Bush. But their quarrel with the American political class predates him, emanating from several policies:

- American support for Israel's occupation of Palestinian lands, the brutal suppression of Palestinian resistance and the 1982 Israeli invasion of Lebanon, which left 15,000 Lebanese and Palestinians dead;
- American alliances with undemocratic and oppressive Muslim — particularly Arab — regimes;
- The 1991-2003 US-led economic sanctions on Iraq that, according to various United Nations agencies, the International Red Cross and a Harvard University study team, caused the slow death of an estimated 1 million Iraqis, half of them children under the age of five.[2] In 1996, Madeleine Albright, US secretary of state, was asked if so high a price was worth the American goal of "regime change" in Baghdad. Her chilling reply: "We think the price is worth it."[3]
- Washington's silence over Russia's two wars on Chechnya (1994-96 and 1999 to date), which killed between 100,000 and 200,000 Muslims.[4]

American humanitarian interventions in Muslim Bosnia (1995) and Kosovo (1999) in the former Yugoslavia, where at least 200,000 Muslims were killed under Serb ethnic cleansing, did generate goodwill. But that has long since been pushed into the background by the anti-Bush backlash. Poll after poll has shown unprecedented Muslim hostility, not toward the American people, but toward the American government.

It did not have to come to this. The September 11 terrorist attack engendered as much sympathy for the US and Americans in the Muslim world as elsewhere. There was a candlelight vigil even in Tehran. The United Nations-approved war on Afghanistan, the base of Osama bin Laden and the al Qaeda terrorist network, was supported by several Muslim states. What turned the tide were Bush's unquestioned backing of Israeli prime

Muslims in the World[5]

There are 1.3 billion Muslims, who constitute one-fifth of the world's population.

Islam is the fastest-growing religion in the world, including in Europe, the US and Canada.

Islam is the second-largest religion after Christianity, which has 1.9 billion adherents.

There are more Muslims than there are Catholics (1.1 billion).

Muslims constitute the religious majority in 54 countries.

There are as many Muslims as there are Chinese people.

There are as many Muslims in China (33 million) as there are Canadians in Canada.

There are almost as many Muslims in Europe (20 million) as there are in Yemen (20 million) or Syria (18 million).

There are more Muslims in Canada (600,000) than there are Greek, Ukrainian, Serb and Russian Orthodox combined (480,000), Presbyterians (410,000), Pentecostals (369,000), Jews (330,000) or Buddhists (300,000).

minister Ariel Sharon's brutal crackdown of the 2000-2003 Palestinian intifadah (uprising), and then the unilateral and illegal war on Iraq despite worldwide opposition.

As most of the world feared then and knows now, Bush — enthusiastically supported by British and Italian prime ministers Tony Blair and Silvio Berlusconi — invaded and occupied oil-rich Iraq under false pretenses by exploiting public fears over Muslim terrorism. When every one of the reasons cited for the war was proven wrong — Saddam was not responsible for 9/11; had no connections to al Qaeda; and had neither nuclear, chemical or biological weapons nor the Scud missiles and pilotless planes to hit anyone — Bush and Blair changed their tune. They had gone to war to get rid of a dictator and bring democracy to the Iraqis.

It is said that Saddam killed at least 500,000 Iraqis during his nearly thirty-year gulag. The United States, Britain and their allies killed double that many in half the time, dating back to the economic sanctions.

Muslims also paid the biggest price for the Bush administration's incompetence. Iraqis got a new constitution and held elections, but they didn't have regular drinking water and electricity, and they couldn't venture out of their homes for fear of being shot dead by anti-American insurgents or by American soldiers in "friendly fire." In Afghanistan, years after the ouster of the Taliban, American relief and reconstruction work remained mired in bureaucracy, inefficiency and waste. The promised rebuilding of the economy proved a mirage, and the most lucrative jobs were either in the service of the warlords or in cultivating poppies, as the country went back to being the world's largest exporter of heroin.

The abused and the tortured at the Abu Ghraib prison in Baghdad, at the detention center at Guantanamo Bay (on the US-controlled northern tip of Cuba) and in other secret

American-run prisons in Afghanistan and around the globe were Muslims. In my travels through the Middle East, South Asia and the Far East, I was struck by how acutely aware Muslims everywhere were about the details of the prison abuses, especially the reported desecration of the Qur'an, the force-feeding of pork and alcohol, and the enforced nudity, masturbation and other transgressions of Muslim religious and cultural norms. These were not isolated incidents carried out by a handful of undisciplined soldiers, as first claimed by the Bush administration, but part of a program to break down the inmates by violating their deeply held religious precepts.

Then there was the Bush administration's policy of "extraordinary rendition" — subcontracting torture abroad. In about 1,000 secret flights, chartered Central Intelligence Agency planes, often flying illegally through Canadian and European air space and using their airports, ferried Muslim suspects to Egypt, Saudi Arabia, Pakistan, Syria, Morocco and Uzbekistan — states that have been condemned by the US State Department for human rights violations.[6] From Malawi to Bosnia, the CIA also carried out "cross-border arrests that verged on kidnappings," according to Human Rights Watch,[7] and flew the captives to foreign jails or Guantanamo Bay or secret CIA-run detention facilities.

Even more damaging to the American image among Muslims has been Washington's overt or tacit support for allies who invoked the war on terrorism as a cover to crack down on Muslim dissidents or Muslim resistance to repressive rule. Waving the anti-terrorism banner, Russia, Israel, China, Uzbekistan and the Philippines intensified repression in Chechnya, the West Bank and Gaza, Zinjiang, the Ferghana Valley and Mindanao Island, respectively.

Within weeks of 9/11, the Bush administration introduced a plan to register non-citizen and non-green cardholders from certain Muslim countries. More than 80,000 responded, including many who had been in the US illegally. About 14,000 were picked out for deportation.[8] Rather than risk arrest, thousands left the country. These people were "not terrorists," said Anthony Romero, executive director of the American Civil Liberties Union, but "had come to the United States for the same reason previous generations of immigrants had, for a better life and for freedom."[9] That is not to say that illegal immigrants should have been allowed to stay, but rather that the government conducted a selective prosecution. There were, after all, nearly 11 million illegal immigrants in the US and 305,000 outstanding deportation orders at that time.

The administration also fingerprinted and questioned 50,000 Muslims from or associated with Syria, Libya, Iran, Iraq and Sudan. In addition, 8,000 were identified by the FBI for "voluntary" interviews that turned out to be "highly coercive," according to Romero; they were questioned about their "bank accounts, mosque attendance and opinion about the US, in violation of their constitutional rights to freedom of speech and religion." No one was found to have had any terrorist connection. By the fall of 2005, of the reported 83,000 people detained in the United States and abroad — most without charge — almost all were Muslims. The number of convictions was about 400, of which only 40 were related to terrorism. About 100 detainees died in custody — 26 of them classified as criminal homicides. Among those arrested was James Yee, a 1990 West Point military academy graduate and a Muslim who was appointed the Muslim chaplain at Guantanamo Bay. He was hounded because he had warned against the mishandling of Muslim prisoners there. In September 2003, he was thrown into solitary confinement and charged with mutiny, sedition, espionage and aiding the enemy.

When all those charges had to be abandoned for lack of evidence, he was slapped with lesser, still trumped-up charges of having porn on his computer and committing adultery. These charges were also dropped in March 2004.[10]

The CIA reportedly captured 3,000 people worldwide, and its "black sites" held 100 *desaparecidos*, as the disappeared of Latin America used to be called. "We invoke the term very decidedly," Carroll Bogert, associate director of Human Rights Watch told me in 2005.

Yet Bush claimed, "We do not do torture" — an assertion that fooled neither the world nor even the US Congress, which finally acted in late 2005 to ban cruel, inhumane and degrading treatment under American detention, anywhere. But Bush stuck to his other formulation, the one he first set out in an address to Congress nine days after 9/11: "Why do they hate us? They hate our democratically elected government. They hate our freedoms, our freedom of religion, our freedom of speech, our freedom to vote and assemble and disagree with each other." The fact is, they hate the United States not for what it stands for, but for what it has done.

Throughout all this, much of the American media echoed the steady drumbeat of the Bush propaganda, producing more jingoism than journalism. Little wonder, then, that even as late as December 2004, when most of the abuses against Muslims were well known, 44 percent of Americans believed in restricting the civil rights of Muslim Americans, according to a nationwide survey by Cornell University.[11]

The Patriot Act (passed in a hurry by Congress after 9/11 and renewed in early 2006) — and similar anti-terrorism legislation approved in Canada, Britain, Australia, India, Mexico and elsewhere — suspended or curtailed civil liberties and swept aside some of our most cherished democratic principles.

In Canada—which takes pride in being the world's only constitutionally multicultural nation—five longtime residents, all of Arab origin, languished in jail without charge for years. Two of them went on long hunger strikes to protest their living conditions—in one case to get winter clothing and slippers for his cold cell and in the other to get medical treatment. As Alexandre Trudeau, son of the late prime minister, told me in 2005 while making a documentary about the five, "It is one thing to say we need to hold them because they are a threat to national security; it is another to be punitive with them. The logic may well be that such harsh conditions are an encouragement for them to voluntarily agree to deportation" — to their native nations of Syria, Egypt, Algeria and Morocco (which all practice torture).

"Voluntary deportation" was what twenty-two Pakistani and Indian Muslim men agreed to after being rounded up in Toronto in 2002 amid sensational accusations of being an al Qaeda sleeper cell that was going to blow up a nuclear facility and the CN Tower, the tallest free-standing structure in the world. But in the end they were only charged with petty immigration violations— not terrorism offenses—and they simply left the country.

Meanwhile, an independent judicial commission in Canada — the only one of its kind in the post-9/11 world — probed American and Canadian complicity in the torture of Ottawa software engineer Maher Arar in a Syrian jail. He was merely passing through New York airport in the fall of 2001 when American security officials, after consulting their Canadian counterparts, put him on a special CIA flight to Damascus, where he was held for 374 days. He was released only after a spirited campaign in Canada by his indefatigable wife, Monia Mazigh, with the help of human rights groups and the opposition New Democratic Party in Parliament. "I never heard of a Canadian being deported to Ireland because of his Irish descent," she told me in 2003. "A Canadian citizen traveling on a Canadian passport must be treated according to Canadian values. If he has done something wrong, charge him." Arar was never charged.

Shortsighted policies have given our democracies a bad name. The moral currency of the United States in particular has been devalued. When the International Red Cross, Amnesty International, Human Rights Watch and other respected human rights organizations lambaste the Bush administration's policies, when the president places himself above the law, when his vice-president and two successive attorneys general try to justify torture by playing with its meaning (it's not torture unless you are dead or near-dead), when the president pressures the government of Qatar, the home base of Al-Jazeera TV, to clamp down on that media because of its critical news coverage of his policies, and when his administration pays to plant positive stories in both the Iraqi and the American media, that president loses the moral right to claim to be exporting democratic values to the Middle East and beyond.

The tragedy of 9/11 divided the world into two broad camps. One camp insisted that it was all about Islam. The other claimed that it was about nineteen criminals. The former succeeded in tarring not only all Muslims with the terrorist brush but Islam as well. This was clearly designed to divert attention away from American foreign policies, a tactic that did not fool Kofi Annan, secretary-general of the United Nations. Speaking to a UN conference on Islamophobia in New York in December 2004, he cited the uprisings in Palestine, Chechnya and other hotspots of the world, and added pointedly, "We should remember that these are political reactions — disagreements with specific policies. All too often, they are mistaken for an Islamic reaction against Western values."[12]

The anti-Islamic intellectual crusade in the US, the UK, Australia and elsewhere continues to alienate Muslims, whose cooperation is essential in combating terrorism. Far worse, it has eroded our pluralistic civility, demeaned our cherished multicultural collectivity and devalued our democracies, while not mak-

Laughing at the Siege

September 11, 2001 changed the world. It also cracked open the market for Muslim comics. Not long after 9/11, the following joke was making the rounds:

Some American Muslims, buoyed by their increasing numbers from immigration and a high conversion rate, used to daydream that, some day, America would become a Muslim nation. And, lo and behold, it did right after 9/11. People were being picked up in the middle of the night without warrants, locked up in secret cells without charge, without a lawyer, without bail, without access to family and friends, and they were subjected to verbal, psychological and physical abuse. America had become a Muslim nation, all right!

Azhar Usman of Chicago, known as the ayatollah of comedy, says, "There's obviously a very strong stereotype that Muslims are a terrorist people; so my act focuses on breaking down those stereotypes." Here's Usman:

"Everyone is very nice to me once the plane lands."

"To non-Muslims, our mosque minarets look like missiles."

"The black man is always complaining that he can't get a fair trial in America. The Muslim says, 'We can't even get a trial!'"

Usman, who with his beard and skullcap looks like a member of the Taliban, and says so, bounds up on stage with the traditional

ing us any safer. In fact, the world has more terrorism than when Bush launched his war on it. "Bring 'em on," he taunted the terrorists. They have come on in droves, especially in Iraq. "You're with us, or against us," he warned the world. Most of it is now ranged against the US.

Muslim greeting of *Assalam-u-alaikum* (peace be with you). "For those of you who don't know what that means, it means, 'We are gonna kill you!'"

Others have their own security-related jokes.

Ahmed Ahmed, an Egyptian American: "I went to the airport. The man behind the check-in counter asked if I packed my bags myself. 'Yes, sir,' I said. They arrested me."

"My name is Shazia Mirza. At least that's what it says on my pilot's license," cracks the most well-known female Muslim comic. The Briton is, like Usman, an observant Muslim who eschews drinking and pre-marital sex. "I never joke about sex — because I've never had it."

Other female comics are also doing well. Tissa Hami of Boston: "Why are there so few female Muslim comics? I didn't want competition, so I stoned them."

Maysoon Zayid, Palestinian American activist, aims this barb at George W. Bush: "It should be the goal of every Arab man to marry one of the Bush twins. And if you are Muslim and Arab, try to marry both."

www.shaziamirza.org
www.azhar.com
www.preachermoss.com
www.maysoon.com
www.tissahami.com

www.ahmed-ahmed.com
www.bootlegislam.com
www.arabcomedy.org
www.somethingspace.com

ISLAMOPHOBIA

The current strain of Islam-bashing bears all the symptoms of racism. It holds up the most marginal and fanatical Muslims, totaling at the most a few thousand, as representatives of all 1.3 billion Muslims. It expects every Muslim to explain or apologize for the actions of the few.

The tendency to see all Muslims as one prompts the media and even governments to demand, Who speaks for Muslims? The answer is that, as with other religions, many groups and organizations do, depending on religious, social or political requirements. The range of Muslim views is, arguably, wider. Muslims come from different regions, races, nations, ethnicities and cultures, speak different languages, follow strict or liberal interpretations of Islam, or don't follow any at all, though they consider themselves Muslim. While a diversity of voices in other religious communities is considered normal, in Muslims it is seen as exasperating proof of divisiveness and disarray.

Another oft-asked question is, Where are the "moderate" Muslims? These are usually defined as those who not only condemn terrorism, but who also agree with the policies of Bush and his allies, and confirm the prevailing prejudices against other Muslims. This handful of Muslims are often courted and quoted by the media. The surest way for a Muslim to get news coverage is to attack fellow Muslims. He or she — ideally someone alienated from Islam due to some personal experience, which is then presented as symptomatic of the Muslim norm — is portrayed as a "reformer," courageous enough to speak out. Some may be. But many are positioning and marketing themselves as such. For them, it is a ticket to prominence.

British author and broadcaster Tariq Ali has observed that while Americans no longer keep House Negroes, they do cultivate House

Arabs and House Muslims.[13] So do some Europeans. And they are using them to lend a patina of credibility to questionable policies. In France, for example, the Jacques Chirac government cited non-hijabi Muslim women to rationalize its ban on *hijab* (headscarf) for schoolgirls. In Canada, the province of Quebec used the sole Muslim member of the National Assembly to lead a symbolic vote against the ostensible introduction of *sharia* (Islamic religious code) in the province of Ontario. What had been asked for was not sharia at all, but religious-based family arbitration for Muslims, available to Christians and Jews since 1991. One can't imagine a government anywhere using a lapsed or dissident Catholic to strip away the rights of practicing Catholics.

This is not to deny anyone freedom of speech. The media also have the right to quote whomever they wish. And governments may be excused for following public opinion rather than leading it. But our public discourse is dangerously distorted, and public policy badly skewed, when the only voices the public is allowed to hear are those of Osama bin Laden and other militants on the one hand and, on the other, those willing to mimic the prejudices of their benefactors. This leaves out 99 percent of Muslims, the very constituency that the West needs to hear from, not only for a better understanding of Islam and Muslims but, more important, to help marginalize the terrorists.

Not only are all Muslims blamed for terrorism, but Islam itself is blamed. Franklin Graham, son of Billy Graham and spiritual adviser to Bush, called Islam "an evil and wicked religion." Evangelist Pat Robertson called it a violent faith. John Ashcroft, Bush's first attorney general, who, like Bush, is a born-again Christian, said that "Islam is a religion in which God requires you to send your son to die for him; Christianity is a faith in which God sends his son to die for you." Jerry Vines of the Southern

Baptist Convention accused the Prophet Muhammad of being "a demon-possessed pedophile."

All this is neither new nor original.

Anti-Islamic views were common in Europe during and after the Christian Crusades against Muslims (1098-1291). Islam was depicted as a religion of the sword, and the Prophet Muhammad was demonized as Mahound, the Prince of Darkness, or the Beast of the Apocalypse. Crude characterizations of Islam and the Prophet were recycled in more muted forms by European colonialists occupying Muslim lands. The bigoted imagery had begun to subside during our contemporary era of pluralism, only to be resurrected with a vengeance after 9/11. Now, instead of the scimitar-wielding warriors, we have "Islamic" terrorists. It is as if Catholicism were responsible for the Irish Republican Army, the Serbian Orthodox Church for Slobodan Milosevic's ethnic cleansing in Bosnia and Kosovo, and American Protestantism for Timothy McVeigh blowing up a federal building in Oklahoma City in 1995.

The Qur'an is being studied for clues to the militant Muslim mind. There was no such rush to buy the Bible or the Torah when some Afrikaners or Serbs or Jewish settlers were justifying their actions in the name of fulfilling their God's mission. Even more instructive of our troubled times is that anti-Islamists are quoting the Qur'an, selectively and out of context, exactly as Osama bin Laden does — they to "prove" that Islam is a militant faith and he to justify his murders. What are we to make of *this* axis of evil?

Islamophobia is not confined to overt bigots. The broader public is complicit in varying degrees. Anti-Islamic screeds are bestsellers in the United States and Europe. And poll after poll has quantified broad-based hostility to Muslims.[14] What is said and tolerated about Muslims would at once be denounced as hate-mongering if applied to other people. Replace the words Muslim and Islam in public pronouncements with Jew and Judaism, or Christian and Christianity, and see how it reads.

Some of the anti-Muslim sentiment is driven by the lack of the most rudimentary knowledge of Islam, as shown by John Kerry, the 2004 Democratic presidential candidate, who called for more international troops in Iraq, "particularly Muslim-speaking and Arab-speaking Muslim troops."[15] Might the US need some Christian-speaking and white-speaking people?

"What we have is not a clash of civilizations but a clash of ignorance," the Aga Khan, spiritual leader of the Ismaili Muslims, told me in 2005. "You can be an educated person in the Judeo-Christian world and know nothing — I mean, nothing — about the Islamic world. The presumption in democracies is that the electorate is capable of commenting on major issues of national or international importance, and that our leaders are educated in the subject matters that they need to know about in order to lead. So, unless there is a better understanding of the Islamic world, democracies are not going to be able to express themselves on Islamic issues."

Much of the present anger at Muslims is clearly rooted in post-9/11 fears and has led to a demonization of Muslims on a scale not seen in modern times. "It is not like the vulgar bigotry against the Japanese in World War II or against the Chinese a century ago; it is more refined, more subtle, highly intellectualized and thus more dangerous," says Khaled Abou El Fadl, professor of law at UCLA. In a 2002 interview with me, he cited four telltale anti-Islamic themes:

"The most insidious is that Muslims have existed fundamentally and irreparably in a state of conflict with the Judeo-

Christian civilization: 'Well, you know it was like that in history and will remain so.'"

The second posits Islam as "a fascist ideology, fundamentally aggressive or totalitarian."

The third is the "sleeper jihad" theory, which triggers the so-called holy war ideology in any Muslim. "Like a keg of dynamite that could explode at any time!"

The fourth theme — and this is the one that Bush uses — is to offer passing praise for Islam as a religion of peace but to attack "political Islam" or "radical Islam" or "Islamism." The faith is fine as long as "it is a completely private creed, practiced solely in the confines of the home. But the moment it wants to engage the world, it is dangerous," El Fadl said. All politically active Muslims can, therefore, be dismissed as fundamentalists, zealots or fanatics. Such bigotry was once confined to a handful of academics and government officials, but now it permeates "many elements of the American intelligentsia and others influential in drawing up legislation, immigration laws and American foreign policy."

Muslims and Muslim nations are often subject to double standards.

United Nations resolutions on Iraq and Syria/Lebanon must be obeyed, but the ones calling on Israel to vacate the Occupied Territories may be ignored.

Political Islam is dangerous, but Zionism, and the political agenda of the American Moral Majority, are not.

Muslim fundamentalism is to be feared, but Christian, Jewish and Hindu fundamentalisms, which have seen a parallel rise, are minor irritants.

Non-violent Muslims dreaming of establishing a worldwide caliphate (rule by an Islamic leader) are problematic, but the 100 million born-again Christian Americans who want a Kingdom of God on Earth are not.

The free distribution of the Qur'an in Central Asia and elsewhere by the oil-rich Arabs is worrisome, but the gifting of the Bible in Iraq or Afghanistan or Sudan by Christian missionaries is not.

Every imprudent word by an *imam* (Islamic cleric), however illiterate or obscure, is to be ferreted out and broadcast to the world, while the fanaticism of the priests of other faiths can go unmonitored.

Just about every case of a woman condemned to some form of sharia punishment in Nigeria or Iran or Pakistan is to be widely publicized, but the ongoing inhumane treatment and deaths of hundreds of thousands of Muslims in the Israeli Occupied Territories, Chechnya, Kashmir, Iraq and Afghanistan are not worthy of political or editorial outrage.

None of this is to say that Muslims do not have problems. They do. But the problems are not quite what Islamophobes make them out to be.

THE MUSLIM MALAISE

He who wrongs a Jew or a Christian will have me as his accuser on the Day of Judgment .

— Prophet Muhammad[16]

One of the strangest aspects of the post-9/11 world is that despite all the talk about Muslim terrorism, there is hardly any exploration of the complex causes of Muslim rage. Muslims *are* in a state of crisis, but their most daunting problems are not religious. They are geopolitical, economic and social — problems that have caused widespread Muslim despair and, in some cases, militancy, both of which are expressed in the religious terminology that Muslim masses relate to.

Most Muslims live in the developing world, much of it colonized by Western powers as recently as fifty years ago. Not all Muslim shortcomings emanate from colonialism and neo-imperialism, but several do.

As part of the spoils of the First World War, Britain and France helped themselves to much of the Ottoman Empire, including Syria, Iraq, Lebanon and what is now Israel, Jordan and the Palestine Authority. In later years, they and other European colonial powers created artificial states such as Kuwait and Nigeria. Or they divided peoples and nations along sectarian lines, such as bifurcating India in 1947 into Muslim Pakistan and largely Hindu India. In more recent years, the United States has maintained repressive proxy regimes in the Middle East to stifle public anti-Israeli sentiments, keep control of oil and maintain a captive market for armaments.

While the past casts a long shadow over Muslims, it is the present that haunts them.

Hundreds of millions live in zones of conflict, precisely in the areas of European and American meddling, past and present — US-occupied Iraq, US-controlled Afghanistan, the Israeli Occupied Territories and Kashmir, the disputed Muslim state on the border of India and Pakistan in the foothills of the Himalayas. Only the Russian war on Muslim Chechnya is not related to the history of Western machinations, but even that has had the tacit support of the Bush administration. These conflicts, along with the economic sanctions on Iraq, have killed an estimated 1.3 million Muslims in the last fifteen years alone. Why are we surprised that Muslims are up in arms?

In addition, nearly 400 million Muslims live under authoritarian despots, many of them Western puppets, whose corruption and incompetence have left their people in economic and social shambles.

It is against this backdrop that one must look at the current malaise of Muslims and their increasing emotional reliance on their faith.

Economic Woes

The total GDP of the fifty-six members of the Islamic Conference, representing more than a quarter of the world's population, is less than 5 percent of the world's economy. Their trade represents barely 7 percent of global trade, even though more than two-thirds of the world's oil and gas lie under Muslim lands. The standard of living in Muslim nations is abysmal even in the oil-rich regions, because of unconscionable gaps between the rulers and the ruled. A quarter of impoverished Pakistan's budget goes to the military. Most of the $2 billion a year of American aid given to Egypt as a reward for peace with Israel goes to the Egyptian military.

The most undemocratic Muslim states, which also happen to be the closest allies of the US, are the most economically backward.

The Arab nations, with a combined population of 280 million, muster a total GDP less than that of Spain. The rate of illiteracy among Arabs is 43 percent, worse than that of much poorer nations. Half of Arab women are illiterate, representing two-thirds of the 65 million Arabs who cannot read or write. About 10 million Arab children are not in school.[17] The most-educated Arabs live abroad, their talents untapped, unlike those of the Chinese and Indian diasporas, who have played significant roles in jump-starting the economies of their native lands.

A disproportionate percentage of the world's youth are Muslim.

Half of Saudi Arabia's and a third of Iran's populations are younger than twenty. There are few jobs for them. "Young and unemployed" is a phenomenon common to many Muslim nations.

A majority of the world's 12 million to 15 million refugees are Muslims, fleeing poverty and oppression. Europe's 20 million Muslims suffer high unemployment and poverty, especially in Germany and France (see European Muslims).

It was inevitable that many Muslims would find comfort in Islam.

Islamic Resurgence

Fundamentalism has been on the rise, and not just in Islam. There has been a parallel rise in Judaism, Christianity, Hinduism, Sikhism and Buddhism, with its inevitable political fallout — in the Israeli settler movement in the Occupied Territories, the politicization of the American conservative right (culminating in the election and re-election of George W. Bush), the rise to power of the Hindu nationalists in India, the Sikh separatist movement in the Punjab in India and the aggressive nationalism of the Sinhalese in Sri Lanka.

That many Muslims have become "fundamentalist" does not mean that they are all fanatic and militant. Nor is the Muslim condition fully explained by the use of petro-dollars. First, Arab financial support for Islamic institutions around the world is still no match for the resources available for Christian global missionary or Zionist political work. Second, and more to the point, the rise of Islam is not confined to areas of Arab financial influence; it is a worldwide phenomenon.

Mosques are full. The use of the *hijab* (headscarf) is on the rise. *Madrassahs* (religious schools) are packed. *Zakat* (Islamic charity) is at record levels, especially where governments have failed to provide essential services. In Egypt, much of the health care, emergency care and education are provided by the Muslim Brotherhood, in the Occupied Territories by Hamas, in Pakistan and elsewhere by groups that may be far less political but are no less Islamic.

With state institutions riddled with corruption and nepotism, some of the most talented Muslims, both rich and poor, have abandoned the official arena and retreated into the non-governmental domain of Islamic civil society.

The empty public sphere has been filled with firebrands — ill-tutored and ill-informed clergy or populist politicians who rally the masses with calls for *jihad* (struggle) for sundry causes. The greater the injustices in Iraq, Afghanistan, the Israeli Occupied Territories, Chechnya or elsewhere, the greater the public support for those calling for jihad. Jihad has also proven to be good business for many a *mullah* (Muslim priest) who has become rich or influential, or both, preaching it. Meanwhile, unelected governments lack the legitimacy and confidence to challenge the militant clerics, and fluctuate between ruthlessly repressing them and trying to out-Islamize them.

To divert domestic anger abroad, many governments also allow and sometimes encourage the radicals to rant at the US and rave at Israel, or just at Jews. Sometimes even the elected leaders join in, as has Iranian president Mahmoud Ahmedinijad, denying the Holocaust and calling for Israel to be "wiped off the map."

In reality, most Muslim states are powerless to address the international crises that their publics want addressed. They have neither the military nor the economic and political clout to matter much to the US, the only power that counts these days. Or, as in the case of Egypt, Jordan and the oil-rich Arab oligarchies, they are themselves dependent on Washington for their own survival.

Feeling abandoned, the Muslim masses find comfort in religion. The Palestinian resistance to Israeli occupation was a secular struggle before it became "Islamic." The same was true of the Lebanese resistance to the Israeli occupation of southern Lebanon, and also of the Chechyn resistance to Russian repression. Similarly, domestic critics of authoritarian regimes have found a hospitable home in the mosque.

Islam being their last zone of comfort, most Muslims react strongly — sometimes irrationally and violently — when their faith or their Prophet is mocked or criticized, as the world witnessed during the Danish cartoon crisis (see European Muslims). They react the way the angry disenfranchised do — hurling themselves into the streets, shouting themselves hoarse and destroying property, without much concern for the consequences, and engendering even more hostility in the West toward Muslims and Islam. But, as the American civil rights leader Martin Luther King famously said, riots are the voice of the voiceless.

Muslims have developed a "siege mentality, which is what the screaming, dogmatic and atavistic clerics" appeal to, says Chandra Muzaffar, Malaysian Muslim human rights activist. As he was telling me this in Kuala Lumpur in 2005, Sharifa Zuriah, a founder of Sisters in Islam, an advocacy group for Malaysian Muslim women, intervened: "Muslims have developed a complex. They think they won't be heard if they don't shout. Every statement is like a war."

Then there is real war, the war of terrorism.

Terrorism's Fallout

"That a majority of Al Qaeda are Muslims is not to say that a majority of Muslims are Al Qaeda, or subscribe to its tenets," Stephen Schulhofer, professor of law at New York University, told me in 2003. But it is also true that most terrorists these days are Muslims. That may only be a function of the times we live in — yesterday's terrorists came from other religions and tomorrow's may hail from some other. Still, terrorism has forced a debate among Muslims, who are divided into two camps. One side says that Muslims should no more have to apologize for their extremists than Christians, Jews or Hindus or anybody else, and that doing so only confirms the collective guilt being placed on Muslims. The other side believes that as long as some Muslims are blowing up civilians in suicide bombings, slitting the throats of hostages and committing other grisly acts, it is the duty of all Muslims to speak out and challenge the murderers' warped theology. The latter view has prevailed. Terrorism — suicide bombings in particular — has been widely condemned.

Just because an overwhelming majority of Muslims condemn Osama bin Laden and other extremists, however, does not mean that they feel any less for Muslims in Iraq or Palestine. Or that the internal debate that he has forced on Muslims is new. Throughout their 1,400-year history, Muslims have argued and quarreled over various interpretations of the Qur'an and religious traditions.

But it *is* a sign of the times that the most extreme interpretation of the Qur'an appeals to Muslim masses these days, and that far too many clerics are attacking Christians and Jews and delivering fire-and-brimstone sermons full of the imagery of war and martyrdom. This is contrary to the message of the Qur'an — *Do not argue with the followers of earlier revelation other than in the most kindly manner* (29:46) [18] — and the teachings of the Prophet Muhammad: "Do not consider me better than Moses," and, "I am closest of all people to Jesus, son of Mary."

For all the emphasis that today's clerics put on the Prophet's war record, he spent a total of less than a week in actual battle in the twenty-three years of his prophethood. He advised his followers to "be moderate in religious matters, for excess caused the destruction of earlier communities." A moderate himself, he smiled often, spoke softly and delivered brief sermons.

"The Prophet disliked ranting and raving," wrote Imam Bukhari, the ninth-century Islamic scholar of the Prophet's sayings. Ayesha, the Prophet's wife, reported that "he spoke so few words that you could count them." His most famous speech, during the Haj pilgrimage in AD 632, which laid down an entire covenant, was less than 2,800 words (see The Sermon that Changed the World).

Muhammad was respectful of Christians and Jews. Hearing the news that the king of Ethiopia had died, he told his followers, "A righteous man has died today; so stand up and pray for your brother." When a Christian delegation came to Medina, he invited them to conduct their service in the mosque, saying, "This is a place consecrated to God." When Saffiyah, one of his wives, complained that she was taunted for her Jewish origins, he told her, "Say unto them, 'my father is Aaron, and my uncle is Moses.'"

Yet angry Muslims, not unlike African Americans not too long ago, pay little heed to voices of moderation. This is partly a reflection of the fact that there is no central religious authority in Islam. Only the minority Shiites have a religious hierarchy of ayatollahs, who instruct followers on religious and sometimes political matters. The majority Sunnis do not have the equivalent of the Pope or the Archbishop of Canterbury. A central tenet of their faith is that there is no intermediary between the believer and God. This makes for great democracy — everyone is free to issue a *fatwa* (religious ruling) and everyone else is free to ignore it. But the "fatwa chaos" does create confusion — among non-Muslims, who are spooked by the red-hot rhetoric, and also among Muslims, who are left wondering about the "right answers" to some of the most pressing issues of the day.

Muslim Apologetics

There are two kinds of Muslim apologetics. The first is denial: there's little or nothing wrong with Muslims, when there clearly is. The second, seen among some Muslims in the West, takes the form of self-flagellation, of apologizing for their faith or distancing themselves from it. To wit:

"Yes, the problem is Islam, and we must fix it." (Why is Islam any more of a problem than any other faith? And how are they going to fix it?)

"I am a Muslim but I am not a fundamentalist Muslim." (Do Christians say, "I am Christian but not an evangelical Christian?")

"I am a Muslim but ashamed to call myself one." (Do all Hindus have to apologize for those few who, in 1992, went on a mosque-ravaging rampage in India?)

Some of these sentiments may be genuinely held. More likely, they reflect the immigrant pathology of catering to majority mores, a new twist on the past practice of immigrants to North America anglicizing their names.

Such defensiveness aside, Muslims do suffer from deeper problems. Many are preoccupied with the minutiae of rituals (Should one wash the bare feet before prayers or do so symbolically over the socks?) at the expense of the centrality of the faith, which is fostering peace, justice and compassion, not just for Muslims but for everyone. Many Muslims are too judgmental of each other, whereas a central tenet of their faith is that it is up to God to judge — *Your Lord knows best who goes astray* (53:30), (also, 6:117, 16:125, 17:94, 28:56, 68:7).

Some Muslims have taken to a culture of conspiracy theories. Hence the notion that Princess Diana did not die in an accident but was killed because the British royal family did not want her to marry Dodi Al Fayed, a Muslim. Or the canard that Jews working at the World Trade Center had advance notice of 9/11.

There is too much of a literalist reading of the Qur'an (a trait, ironically, also adopted by anti-Islamists in the West). There is too little *ijtehad* (religious innovation) as called for by Islam to keep believers in tune with their times. Theological rigidity and narrow-mindedness have led, among other things, to Sunni hostility toward the minority Shiites, as seen in the sectarian killings in Pakistan.

Muslims complain about the West's double standards, yet they have their own. While they often criticize the United States and Europe for mistreating Muslims, they rarely speak up against the persecution of non-Muslims by Muslims. They also show a high tolerance for Muslims killing fellow Muslims. The Sudanese genocide of the non-Arab Muslims of Darfur drew mostly silence. The killing of Shiites by the Sunnis in Iraq was shrugged off as part of the anti-US resistance. The overt and subtle racism of the oil-rich Arab states toward the millions of their guest workers goes unmourned.

Muslims do not have much to be proud of in the contemporary world. So they take comfort in their burgeoning numbers. At the turn of the millennium in 2000, there were many learned papers projecting the rise in Muslim population. But if Muslims have not achieved much at 1.3 billion, they are not likely to at 1.5 billion, either.

To escape the present, many Muslims hark back to their glorious past: how Islam was a reform movement; how Muslims led the world in knowledge, in astronomy, chemistry, mathematics, medicine, natural sciences, philosophy and physics; and how the Islamic empires were successful primarily because, with some egregious exceptions, they nurtured the local cultures and respected the religions of their non-Muslim majority populations. This is why Egypt and Syria remained non-Muslim under Muslim rule for 300 years and 600 years, respectively, and India always remained majority Hindu.

As true as all that history is, it is not very helpful today unless Muslims learn something from it — to value human life; accept each other's religious differences; respect other faiths; return to their historic culture of academic excellence, scientific inquiry and economic self-reliance; and learn to live with differences of opinion and the periodic rancorous debates that mark democracies.

It may be unfair to berate ordinary Muslims, given that too many are struggling to survive, that nearly half live under authoritarian regimes where they can speak up only on pain of being incarcerated, tortured or killed, and that they are helpless spectators to the sufferings of fellow Muslims in an unjust world order. Yet Muslims have no choice but to confront their challenges, for *Allah never changes a people's state unless they change what's in themselves* (13:11).

Chapter 2
European Muslims

A DEN OF DISCRIMINATION

*We are confronted with the crisis of national identity in
Europe because of globalization and the European Union,
and we tend to blame Islam to avoid discussing it.*
— French author Olivier Roy[1]

Islam is Europe's second-biggest religion. The most common
name conferred in the maternity wards of the three largest cities
in the Netherlands is Muhammad, which is also the fifth most
common name given to new babies in Britain.[2] Yet the continent's 25 million Muslims seem doubly condemned — as immigrants and as Muslims.

Historic European prejudices against Muslims have been
exacerbated by the 2001 attacks on the US, the 2004 train bombing in Madrid and the 2005 subway bombings in London. The
twin European pathologies of xenophobia and Islamophobia
have come together in a toxic mix. Even when Muslims are not
immigrants — two in five have been born in Europe — they are
treated as foreigners. Muslims in France and Germany face the
most systemic discrimination — in citizenship laws, employment
and politics, at school and in day-to-day social contacts.

Unemployment among French Muslims is nearly double the
national average of 9 percent. It is more than 30 percent in the

banlieues, the crowded social housing projects that were the scene of month-long riots in the fall of 2005. The jobless rate for French Muslim university graduates is 26.5 percent, compared to the national average of 5 percent.[3] Unemployment and under-employment extends to the second- and third-generation off-spring of post-Second World War immigrants, mostly the *pieds-noirs* (those who were welcomed into France because they had fought for France in its colonial wars), or guest workers from North Africa (who were invited because of labor shortages). That soccer star Zinedine Zidane rose from their ranks does not mask the mass poverty of millions or the racism that they encounter.

In Germany, the jobless rate for Muslims (mostly Turks) is twice the national average of 11 percent. It is as high as 50 per-cent for younger Muslims in some cities. Schoolchildren of Turkish origin are routinely channeled into dead-end non-aca-demic streams, the way Muslim children are in France.[4]

Job discrimination against Muslims is rampant even in Sweden, despite its liberal views toward immigrants. In Italy and Spain, the gravity of the situation can only be guessed at because most Muslims there do not have citizenship.

The irony is that Europe, with an aging population and a low birthrate, faces a population drop, from 450 million now to 400 million by 2050, unless it attracts new immigrants.[5] There will not be enough working-age people to pay for health care, pen-sions and other benefits. The young that Europe does have in abundance are the urban Muslim underclass, whose working years are being wasted. Germany, with the lowest birthrate in Europe, and France, with the largest number of Muslims on the continent, will find it particularly difficult to fix their ailing economies without making their Muslim youth more productive. More ominously, Europe risks losing some of its angry alienated

Muslims in Europe

Estimated Total: 20 million

Albania: 2.5 million

Austria: 345,000

Belgium: 400,000

Bosnia / Herzegovina: 1.6 million

Britain: 1.6 million

Bulgaria: 110,000

Croatia: 60,000

Cyprus: 140,000

Denmark: 180,000

France: 4 million to 5 million

Germany: 3.3 million

Greece: 140,000

Italy: 500,000

Macedonia: 346,000

Netherlands: 900,000

Serbia — Montenegro: 405,000

— Kosovo: 1.8 million

Slovenia: 50,000

Spain: 500,000

Sweden: 300,000

Switzerland: 310,000

Note: Some European nations, such as France, do not count populations by religious affiliation. Estimates of Muslim populations therefore, vary. The total 20 million figure represents the lower range.

youth to the certainty and the instant identity of Islamic militancy.

Jytte Klausen, professor of political science at Brandeis University, sees a direct relationship between restrictive citizenship laws and the economic, social and political isolation of Muslims. She studied Muslims in six nations (France, Germany, Britain, the Netherlands, Sweden and Denmark) and found that the higher the hurdles to citizenship, the worse the Muslim plight and the slower their integration.[6]

It was not until 2000 that Germany allowed Turks to take up citizenship, even though they had been residents for decades. In France, even those born in the country must pass an acculturation test at eighteen to determine suitability for citizenship based on knowledge of the French language and French culture. "If the Muslims say they pray regularly, the officials take that as *prima facie* evidence that the applicants are not French enough and reject them," Professor Klausen told me in a 2005 interview. Whereas the cornerstone of the French model is that everyone living legally in France is French, regardless of religion or ethnicity, the children of immigrants, especially Muslims from North Africa, are not considered French precisely because of their religion and ethnicity.

France, Germany and Denmark, which have the lowest percentage of their Muslim populations on their electoral rolls, also have the fewest elected Muslim officials. In 2005, France had only three Muslims in the 331-member senate and none from the mainland in the 577-seat National Assembly (its sole Muslim member being from one of France's overseas territories). By contrast, in Britain and the Netherlands, where half the Muslim population is eligible to vote, Muslims enjoy high political representation: Britain (four MPs and seven Lords) and the Netherlands (nine MPs). Sweden, despite its small Muslim population, has five Muslim MPs, because refugees are allowed to obtain citizenship after five years of residency. The equation is clear: no citizenship equals no voting power, equals no political clout, equals marginalization.

Muslim baiting, once the preserve of right-wing parties and leaders, such as Jean-Marie Le Pen in France and the late Pim Fortuyn in the Netherlands, has entered the mainstream. German chancellor Angela Merkel, Italian prime minister Silvio Berlusconi, former French president Valery Giscard d'Estaing and others have been openly anti-Muslim, especially in the context of the possible entry of Muslim Turkey into the European Union. The public discourse on Muslims, besides being indisputably negative, is often misleading and dishonest.

Politicians and media outlets routinely suggest that Muslims may be too religious to integrate. But a 2005 poll by the US State Department showed that barely 1 percent of French Muslims want to remain isolated, while an overwhelming majority want to belong; two-thirds speak French at home; and six in ten do not mind intermarriage.[7] Jytte Klausen found the three hundred Muslim leaders she interviewed to be "overwhelmingly secular in outlook and supportive of core liberal values" but facing enormous hurdles to integration.

European Muslims are also accused of being the recipients of (and hence unduly influenced by) foreign funding, a code word for petro-dollars from Saudi Arabia; or of being under the sway of radical foreign-born imams; or, more sensationally, of being the advance guard of the "Islamic re-conquest of Europe."

Far from being flush with money, most mosques in Europe are struggling. I have been to several in the back alleys of poor neighborhoods or out in the industrial zones in Germany, Spain,

France and elsewhere. Many had to overcome neighborhood objections that were often couched in terms of zoning regulations. Once up and running, most mosques barely make a go of it financially, managing only with much volunteer help.

A study by a domestic French security agency, leaked to the media in 2005, found that Saudi Arabia was financing only a dozen imams who, in fact, were not Saudi citizens.[8] The troublesome clerics across Europe have not been the dreaded Saudis but the so-called freelancers of various nationalities who set up their own mosques or associations, about two dozen in all. It is they who have been in the news with fiery sermons or connections to terrorists. When such imams are charged or deported, European Muslims cheer because they are as repelled as anyone else by these clerics. The main criticism of the deportations has come not from Muslims but from civil libertarians, rightly concerned about due process.

It also turns out that the biggest foreign presence in the mosques are the imams sent from Turkey, Algeria and Morocco under longstanding agreements with the German, French and Dutch governments. Turkey dispatches about 1,200 a year and wants to get out of the business of paying for them. The imam of the main mosque in Paris has been an Algerian paid for by the Algerian government, much to the annoyance of many French Muslims. But the French and other European governments prefer these visiting clerics who, being on the payroll of friendly and generally authoritarian governments, toe the line and pose little danger of becoming the voice of the voiceless. Contrary to popular belief, European Muslims would rather not have foreign clerics but local ones, trained at European universities and seminaries by Islamic experts.

Another disconcerting development has been the growing

sentiment in Germany that sermons in mosques should be delivered not in Turkish but in German — ironic, given that Germany and other European nations have been pressing Turkey to grant the Turkish Kurds their basic human right to use their Kurdish language.

The most hypocritical accusation against Muslims is that they do not respect the separation of church and state, when it is the European states that don't. The Church of England remains the official religion in Britain, even if as a hangover of history. Germany and France have long provided funding for both Catholic and Protestant churches, Christian denominational schools and cemeteries. In the case of Germany, the subsidy runs to 18.5 billion Euros a year.[9]

These examples point to the double jeopardy at work. Most European nations not only keep their Muslim minorities on the political, economic and social margins but also blame them for being there. This is reminiscent of the colonial tactic of telling the colonized that they had only themselves to blame for their subjugated status.

Anti-Islamic prejudice also shows up in the resistance to Turkey joining the European Union. Turkey's relative poverty and its huge and younger population of 72 million do raise the specter of an influx of cheap labor and arouse understandable insecurity among workers, especially in the shrinking industrial sector. But there is no doubt that religious bigotry was a key factor in the 2004 referendum defeat of the EU draft constitution in France and the Netherlands. The results prompted some governments and politicians to give their anti-Turkish position a patina of democracy, saying they were only reflecting the sentiments of their electorates. We can be certain that if the same voters had been displaying anti-Catholic bigotry, French and Dutch leaders would not have pandered to them. It is not just the politicians playing the anti-Muslim card. Even Pope Benedict XVI has made it perfectly clear that "it would be a mistake" to embrace Muslim Turkey, because it "has always represented a different continent, in contrast to (Christian) Europe."[10] Challenged later, he insisted, "Turkey should seek its future among Islamic organizations, not in the Christian-rooted Europe."[11]

Combine the treatment of Muslims in Europe with the European resistance to Turkey and you get the uneasy feeling that Europe is sitting on a time bomb. It is a situation that can only be diffused, as the Swiss Islamic scholar Tariq Ramadan has often pointed out, by acknowledging that Islam is as much a religion of Europe as Christianity and Judaism, that Muslims are also European, that there is no dichotomy in being Muslim and European any more than there is in being Jewish and European, that Muslims are there to stay, and that they deserve no less in terms of basic human rights than their fellow citizens.[12]

RUSHDIE TO VAN GOGH TO CARTOONS

It goes without saying that the 2004 murder of Dutch filmmaker Theo van Gogh in retaliation for his anti-Islamic documentary *Submission*, about the mistreatment of Muslim women, was shocking; that his artistic collaborator Ayaan Hirsi Ali should not have to live under 24-hour police protection; and that the 1989 *fatwa* of death by Ayatollah Ruhollah Khomeini against Salman Rushdie for his book, *The Satanic Verses*, was a call for medieval jungle justice. It was the duty of civilized peoples everywhere to stand steadfast with Rushdie and force Tehran ultimately to recant the fatwa. The Dutch police also deserve kudos for apprehending van Gogh's murderer, and the courts for sentencing him to life imprisonment.

But — yes, there is a but — there is a debate in democracies over whether freedom of expression has limits. It does in countries that have anti-hate laws. Even those that don't legislate limits have their own notions of what is and is not acceptable. It seems that the self-restraint normally exercised in challenging the sacred is more readily abandoned in dealing with Islam. The attacks on Islam and Muhammad are, arguably, more persistent, more inflammatory and more vulgar than those against other faiths and other prophets.

In the Rushdie novel, the prostitutes were named after the wives of the Prophet Muhammad, and their customers drew pleasure because they were the wives of "Mahound," the derogatory name given the Prophet by post-Crusades Europe. In van Gogh's documentary, a verse from the Qur'an was projected onto a woman's naked body — "a man may take his woman in any manner, time or place ordained by God" — leaving the impression that God decreed women to be the chattel of men. In fact, Islam ended the treatment of women as property.

To the West, the van Gogh and Rushdie cases proved the murderous irrationality of Muslims. To most Muslims, it showed how incendiary some can be in vilifying Islam.

Then there was the Danish cartoon controversy, the broad outlines of which are by now familiar. A Danish publisher reported having trouble finding an artist to illustrate a children's book about Prophet Muhammad, given Islam's prohibition against depicting him. *Jyllands-Posten*, the conservative mass-circulation daily, commissioned forty illustrators to defy the ban. Of the dozen drawings it published on September 30, 2005, the one that acquired the most notoriety depicted the prophet as a terrorist with bulging eyes and a bomb-shaped turban with a burning fuse. Another showed him as a crazed, knife-wielding

Bedouin. Another placed him at the gates of heaven telling suicide bombers, "Stop. Stop. We have run out of virgins!"

This drew understandable protests from Danish Muslims — at 180,000, the second-largest religious group after the Lutheran Protestants. But they were ignored, both by the newspaper and the government. They sent delegations to the Middle East to lobby other Muslims, a perfectly legitimate exercise. Airing one's domestic dirty laundry abroad is the last resort of the marginalized — used, among others, by the aboriginal peoples of Canada to embarrass Canadians into behaving better toward them.

The delegations carried not only the published cartoons but also other more poisoned ones that were in circulation in Denmark. They said they never passed off the latter as the former. Including the unpublished drawings, too, was legitimate; after all, they did exist.

The lobbying efforts took time to catch on, as often happens with public grievances, especially by a marginalized group with few resources. Eventually, the Arab League and the Islamic Conference, the 56-member umbrella organization of Muslim nations, protested.

A grassroots consumer boycott of Danish products, another legitimate form of peaceful protest, spread from Saudi Arabia across the Persian Gulf. Arla Foods, the Danish dairy, said sales came to a "standstill." Other Danish firms reported lost sales. In Copenhagen, the Confederation of Danish Industries accused *Jyllands-Posten* of jeopardizing $1 billion in annual sales, prompting a disingenuous apology from the editors: "We are sorry *if Muslims have been offended*" (my emphasis).

Soon there were mass Muslim demonstrations around the world, and some turned violent and ugly. Danish flags were burnt, a few Danish embassies torched. This caused much consternation in the West. "What's wrong with Muslims?" "Can't they take a few offensive cartoons in their stride?" "And why must they resort to violence?"

No grievance justifies violence. But the biggest victims were Muslims themselves — nearly fifty dead, shot by anti-riot police in Afghanistan and elsewhere. That speaks to the Muslim pathology of self-inflicted wounds. But the anger in the West was not over the Muslim dead but over the damage caused to Danish embassies. Such selective outrage bespoke prejudice, not principle.

The editors of *Jyllands-Posten*, and the other publications that reprinted the cartoons in an act of solidarity, invoked freedom of speech, of course. But it is not an unfettered right. It is circumscribed by laws of libel, hate and religious freedom.

In February 2006, notorious British historian David Irving was sentenced to three years for denying the Holocaust, and radical British Muslim cleric Abu Hamza al Masri was jailed for, among other things, inciting hatred. It was about time. Yet there were few protests against the curtailment of their freedom of speech. How does a democracy decide which hate is worse?

A few months earlier in France, the Catholic Church won a lawsuit against a fashion designer who had depicted *The Last Supper* with semi-nude women instead of the apostles. Where were the advocates of freedom of speech then? Or do they pop up only to claim the right to bash Muslims?

Beyond the restrictions imposed by law, there is self-restraint. Newspapers and magazines routinely reject cartoons that may be unfair or unnecessarily hurtful or racist. That's why we no longer see the caricatures of savage aboriginals, fat-lipped blacks, hook-nosed Jews or cross-eyed Chinese. That's why even *Jyllands-Posten* would not smear its pages with anti-Semitic graffiti or drawings that might depict the Pope, say, in semi-nude gay poses or consorting with a mistress. And had the paper been foolish enough to do so, we can be certain that not many people would have rushed to its defense. As it turned out, the newspaper did reject caricatures of Christ three years ago, saying they were offensive and "will provoke an outcry."

The lesson Muslims drew from the cartoon episode was that for many in the West, freedom of speech meant mostly the freedom to malign Muslims. This sentiment was summed up in a cartoon in the *Al-Quds al-Arabi*, the pan-Arab daily from London, showing an artist at work at *Jyllands-Posten*. In the first panel, he rejects a grotesque drawing of a black person: "This is racism." He rejects the second, which equates the Star of David with the swastika: "This is anti-Semitism." He keeps the longer third panel, of the Prophet's cartoons, saying: "This is freedom of speech."

This issue of double standards is at the heart of the repeated conflicts between the West and the world of Islam over how far anti-Islamic provocateurs can go in baiting Muslims, secure in the knowledge that they will get away with it. In the Danish case, they didn't. Our inconsistencies finally caught up to us.

That was not all the cartoon controversy exposed. The debate on the issue revealed two overriding aims: minimize the offense caused or discredit the Muslim response. As Gary Younge, the New York-based black British columnist, wrote in *The Nation*: "Muslims have been vilified twice: once through the original cartoons and then again for having the gall to protest them. Such logic recalls the words of the late South African black nationalist Steve Biko: 'Not only are whites kicking us, they are telling us how to react to being kicked.'"[13]

It was said that the ban on depicting Muhammad couldn't be all that serious since there have been drawings of him in the past.

Early artists did draw Muhammad in various scenes but only a few showed his face, while others blanked it out. These can be seen in the Topkapi Palace Library in Istanbul and other collections. But some centuries ago Muslims came to a consensus against depicting the Prophet, lest it lead to idolatry, a sin in Islam. That consensus holds. Non-Muslims can no more mock that belief than Muslims can question some article of Christian or Jewish or Hindu faith.

It was said that Muslims were trying to force non-Muslims to live by Islamic taboos. Not so. Muslims in the West were only asking that democracies live up to democratic values, namely, the laws and mores governing freedom of speech. The cartoon debate had little or nothing to do with blasphemy, either. Some Muslims may have invoked it but that's a tangent democracies need no longer follow. The real issue is that freedom of speech has limits. PEN International, the writers' group that is also a leading advocate of freedom of speech, speaks in its charter to the "unhampered transmission of thought." But it also insists that "since freedom implies voluntary restraint, members pledge themselves to oppose such evils of a free press as mendacious publication, deliberate falsehood and distortion of facts for political and personal ends." It calls on PEN members to foster "good understanding and mutual respect among nations... to do their utmost to dispel race, class and national hatreds, and to champion the ideal of one humanity living in peace in the world."

It was said that the cartoons had offended only the "extremists" or "fundamentalists." No. The offence was broadly felt, even though only some took to the streets. Critics included such "moderates" as Hosni Mubarak, president of Egypt, and Hamid Karza, president of Afghanistan. Some media approvingly quoted a few Muslims as saying that the cartoons had not offended them. But invoking them is like citing a handful of dissident Jews to say what most Jews should believe.

It was said by President Bush and others that some foreign governments — Iran and Syria, in particular — had instigated the protests. Doesn't Bush also manipulate the public? Besides, the worst protests took place in US-controlled Afghanistan and US-friendly Pakistan, Libya and the Israeli Occupied Territories.

It was said that the controversy confirms doubts about whether Muslim immigrants can be integrated in Europe. In Canada and the United States, we used to express just such doubts about Catholics, Jews, Chinese, Japanese, Italians and other "unassimilable groups" — about a hundred years ago. We now see it for what it is: nativist bigotry.

It was said that Arabs/Muslims were being hypocritical in criticizing the cartoons since they routinely demonize Israel, even Jews. I said so myself initially. But later I thought it to be an argument of perfunctory value. It says, in effect, "Since they do it, we can do it, too." No, we ought to conduct ourselves by our democratic standards.

It was said, by the editors of *Jyllands-Posten* and those defending them, that the paper did not mean to offend Muslims. Really? It is a populist paper catering to anti-immigrant and anti-Muslim prejudices. Here's Flemming Rose, the editor who commissioned the drawings, talking about Danish Muslims: "People are no longer willing to pay taxes to help support someone called Ali who comes from a country with a different language and culture that's 5,000 miles away."[14]

It was said that liberal Denmark didn't deserve to be tarnished. But it *is* a hotbed of intolerance toward Muslims. In no other European Union country is there so much xenophobia and hostility toward Islam, according to the European Network

Against Racism. Queen Margrethe has stated that there's "something scary" about the "totalitarianism that's part of Islam." Prime Minister Anders Fogh Rasmussen's parliamentary coalition partner, the People's Party, has called Muslims "cancer cells," "seeds of weeds" and "a plague on Europe."[15] The party also displays paranoia: "Muslim immigration is a way for Muslims to conquer us, just as they have done for the past 1,400 years." "All countries in the West are infiltrated by Muslims. They are nice to us until they are enough to kill us."[16]

The Rushdie, van Gogh and Danish cartoon issues show that the West and the world of Islam are no longer planets apart in this global village. What we say about each other has repercussions, both worldwide and in the West, especially given the presence of millions of Muslim citizens in Europe, North America and Australia. How the West conducts itself toward Muslims is a test of its pluralistic civility, cosmopolitan collectivity and the most fundamental principles of democracy.

THE HIJAB DEBATE

A head covering on a Muslim is a political statement but it is not when on a Christian nun's head.
— Riem Spielhaus, Humboldt University[17]

A simple scarf. That's all a hijab is. Yet it has had the power to unnerve Europe, and parts of the Muslim world. In some Islamic nations, women must wear it even if they don't want to. In parts of Europe and in Turkey and Uzbekistan, schoolgirls and teachers must remove it even if they want to keep it.

There's something about this small piece of cloth that unnerves democrats and despots alike. The hijabi woman has been the target of fascist and feminist as well as racist and religious wrath. She is victimized by those wanting to subjugate her or liberate her. She is the battleground on which anti- and pro-Islamic ideological armies wage wars.

In 1925, Kamal Ataturk, founder of modern Turkey, banned the hijab. That was his idea of secularism.

In 1936, Reza Shah of Iran did so, ordering police to rip the hijab off the heads of women. That was his way of Europeanizing Iranians.

In 1998, Turkey did not let an elected member of parliament take her seat and even stripped her of her citizenship because of her hijab. That was its way of separating state and religion.

In 2002, several German states banned the hijab for teachers. That was their idea of protecting German identity.

In 2003, France banned the hijab for schoolgirls. That was its way of securing French secularism.

In 2004, Uzbekistan, ruled by the tyrant Islam Karimov, started harassing and arresting hijabi women. That was his way of controlling "fundamentalism."

Rulers of a different sort, such as the Taliban in Afghanistan or the mullahs in Iran, decreed the opposite: women had to be veiled, or they would be whipped or jailed. That was their idea of Islam.

French and German restrictions on the hijab are based on the same logic as those of Ataturk and the first shah. The two democracies see secularism the way the despots did: as anti-religious — in this case, anti-Islamic — rather than as a neutral guarantor of religious freedoms for all citizens.

France camouflaged its hijab ban in the rhetoric of rejecting all "ostentatious" religious symbols, including the crucifix and the yarmulke, the Jewish skullcap for men. But no one was fooled. Secularist author Guy Coq said the ideals of the 1789

French Revolution had to be safeguarded: "If we bow to demands to allow the practice of religion in state institutions, we will put the French identity in peril."[18] But no sooner had he hit that high note of principle than he slipped into the abyss of prejudice by clarifying his real target: "To disarm fundamentalism, notably Islamic fundamentalism, can we give up *laïcité*?" But the principle of *laïcité*, the separation of state and religion, was compromised long ago by state subsidies to Christian and Jewish separate schools.

Luc Ferry, French education minister in 2003, positioned the hijab ban as a tool for battling anti-Semitism. But French anti-Semitism is too historic, deep-rooted and widespread to be placed at the feet of teenaged Muslim girls.

In Germany, some regional governments were at least honest in targeting Muslims. One said that all schoolchildren must simply "learn the roots of Christian religion and European culture." Others covered it in half-baked assertions: the *hijab* is a symbol of Islamic oppression; or the exact opposite, an icon of an assertive political Islam.

Muslims themselves have been divided on the subject (see The Qur'an and the Hijab). Hundreds of millions of Muslim women do not wear the hijab. But that's no argument for denying the right of those who want to wear it. That a majority of Christians do not go to church on Sundays does not negate the right of those who do. That a majority of Jews are not Orthodox does not derogate from the fundamental religious rights of those who wear the yarmulke and keep long locks. That some Sikhs shave off their beards and cut their hair does not mean that others do not have the right to believe that their religion commands otherwise. The state, especially a democratic one, has no business dictating which version of a religion should prevail.

The best approach, from an Islamic as well as a secular point of view, is that the matter be left to the individual woman. That is the principle feminists advocated and Western democracies eventually adopted in dealing with abortion.

The only sound public policy is to accept the hijab in public spaces, such as educational institutions and offices, as is the case in Britain, Canada and the US. The state should be active in combating discrimination against hijabi women. It should prosecute employers who refuse to hire or promote hijabi women in accordance with their skill. The government should act as a model employer by hiring qualified hijab-wearing women, as Britain does for its police and immigration departments. This is a natural evolution of the policy enacted earlier for the Jewish yarmulke and the Sikh turban, despite initial pockets of resistance.

As part of its campaign to restore human rights and join the European Union, Turkey is easing the ban on the hijab, and may lift it altogether for women on the public payroll. It is shameful that while the legacy of the autocrat Ataturk is being dismantled in his homeland, part of it is being implemented in Europe.

Hijab: General term for a headscarf of varying lengths and shapes.

Burqa: The head-to-toe outer garment of various shapes and colors, with an opening only for the eyes, dictated by the Taliban in Afghanistan and still worn by some women there, as well as in Pakistan and India. The garment is also known as *abaya* (in Iraq and Saudi Arabia), *chador* (in Iran), *charshaf* (in Turkey) and *jilbab* or *milaya* (in Egypt).

Chapter 3
The Faith

A LIVING FAITH

Grilling Muslims in terrorism-related probes, police tend to ask about the suspect's religiosity, "How often do you pray?" Covering the post-9/11 world, the media make mosque-going sound like a subversive activity. Looking at the passport of a Muslim, airport immigration officials perk up if they see Saudi Arabian stamps of arrival and departure. Examining a Muslim's bank records, security police look suspiciously at any foreign transaction. Listening to a Muslim express solidarity with fellow Muslims everywhere, xenophobes think the worst.

Seen this way, most Muslims can be deemed dangerous. After all, hundreds of millions do pray every day and go to mosques. As many as 4.5 million go to Saudi Arabia every year, either for the pilgrimage of Haj or to visit the holy sites; many of those pilgrims are Americans, Canadians, Europeans and Australians. Millions of Muslims routinely send money to family and friends around the world for charities or for direct distribution to the poor. Most Muslims pray regularly for Muslims caught in wars, invasions and occupations.

All these activities are part and parcel of the ethos of Islam, flowing from the five fundamentals of the faith:

1) Declaration of faith
2) Daily prayers
3) Charity
4) Fasting from sunrise to sunset for one month every year
5) Pilgrimage to Mecca and Medina once in one's lifetime

DECLARATION OF FAITH
Shahada (testimony)

"There is no Allah but Allah, and Muhammad is Allah's messenger." That twin declaration is the first tenet of Islam. That's what Muslims proclaim from childhood and that's how a convert to Islam announces his or her new religious life.

Unlike Hindus, who believe in many gods, Muslims are monotheists. Like Christians and Jews, they believe in one God. But unlike Christians, they do not believe in the Trinity—Father, Son and Holy Spirit. Allah has no associates. Allah is simply the Arabic name for God, used by Arab Christians as well. Allah is the Arabic equivalent of Elohim and Yahweh, the Hebrew names for God, or Jehovah.

Contrary to American evangelist Franklin Graham's post-9/11 assertion that Islam is "not of the same God" as Christianity, it is. Islam is a continuation of Judaism and Christianity. The Qur'an says, *In matters of faith, He has ordained for you that which He has enjoined upon Abraham, Moses and Jesus* (42:13).

Muslims—literally, those who submit—believe Muhammad (born in AD 570) to be Allah's last prophet and messenger. They consider Allah's revelation to him, the Qur'an, to be the last of the revealed books, the earlier ones being the Suhuf (the books) revealed to Abraham but since lost; the Tawrat (Torah) to Moses; the Zabur (Psalms) to David; and the Injil (Gospels) to Jesus.

Jews, Christians and Muslims are thus "peoples of the book" — religious cousins. Two-thirds of the Qur'anic chapters allude to the Bible and mention Adam, Abraham, Moses, David, Solomon and Jesus, referring to them by their Arabic names Aadam, Ibrahim, Moosa, Daood, Sulaiman and Issa, respectively. The Qur'an refers to Ibrahim as *the leader of mankind* (2:124) and tells Muslims that *the faith of your father Ibrahim is your faith* (22:78). Moses, the most mentioned prophet in the Qur'an, is given an exalted status: *O Moosa, I have chosen thee above all mankind* (7:144). An entire chapter, entitled Mariam (Mary), deals with her and Issa (Jesus). The Qur'an confirms the virgin birth. Muhammad said that all "prophets are half-brothers, whose *deen* [faith] is the same but whose *shari'a* [laws] are different."

To Christians, Jesus was the son of God and part of God. To Muslims, Prophet Muhammad was a human being. He was not divine. He is adored and emulated, but it is only Allah that Muslims worship. Islam is not Muhammadenism, and should never be referred to as such. Islam means submission (to Allah), and Muhammad is merely its and his messenger. When upon his death on June 8, 632, some distraught believers refused to accept that reality, Abu Bakr, one of his closest companions, reminded them, "O people! Whoso has been wont to worship Muhammad, he is dead; whoso has been wont to worship Allah, He is living and dies not."[1]

DAILY PRAYERS
Salah or Salat (supplication)

Muslims pray five times a day — before dawn (*Fajr*), past noon (*Zuhr*), late in the afternoon (*Asr*), at dusk (*Maghrib*) and about an hour and a half after sunset (*Isha*).

The Qur'an mentions *salah* about 700 times. *Be steadfast in prayer (29:45). Fortify yourself with patience and prayer; this may indeed be an exacting discipline but not to the devout (2:45). The salah is made obligatory for the believers, to be offered at fixed times* (4:103). And so on.

Prophet Muhammad said, "Salah is the key to Paradise." And he laid down the details of the rituals: "Pray as you have seen me pray."

Prayers are designed to raise God-consciousness five times a day, throughout one's life. Prayers also provide regular exercise — like yoga or Tai Chi or Qigong built into the day — and serve as a calming retreat from the daily demands of life. Muslims thus learn to balance *deeni wa dunyavi* (the spiritual and the worldly). They can't abandon one for the other; that's the essence of their faith.

Muslims come to salah in a state of physical cleanliness. They perform the *wudu* (ablution), which involves the washing of hands, mouth, face and feet. If no water is available, they cleanse themselves symbolically by pressing their open hands against a wall or clean ground, dusting them off and using them to wipe their face and arms up to the elbows. Muslims wear clean clothes when praying. "Cleanliness is half the faith," said the Prophet. Emulating him further, they may wear perfume and avoid eating garlic or onions before going to a mosque.

Muslims may pray individually or, preferably, in a congregation, which is easier in Muslim nations with many neighborhood mosques, or *masajid* (plural of *masjid*, a place of prostration).

Every congregational prayer in the mosque is preceded by the *adan* (the call to prayers), delivered aloud from the mosque minaret or through a loudspeaker. But in nations where the noise bylaws do not permit it (even while allowing church bells to toll) the adan is recited inside the mosque. The words are always the same, sung melodiously by those trained in Arabic incantations and voice projection:

Allah is the greatest, Allah is the greatest
Allah is the greatest, Allah is the greatest
I declare that there's no God except Allah, I declare that
*   there's no God except Allah*
I declare that Muhammad is the messenger of Allah, I
*   declare that Muhammad is the messenger of Allah*
Come for the salah, Come for the salah
Come for success, Come for success
Allah is the greatest, Allah is the greatest
There is no God but Allah.

For the pre-dawn *adan*, another line is added and announced twice: *Salah is better than sleep, Salah is better than sleep.*

Where there's no mosque in the neighborhood, or there is but it cannot broadcast the adan, Muslims keep track of the prayer timings themselves. The noon, afternoon and late-night prayers are easy enough to discern, but the morning and dusk prayers must coincide with the changing times of the rising and setting of the sun. (The *Toronto Star*, Canada's largest newspaper, gets complaints from Muslim readers if it inadvertently omits the sunrise and sunset times from the daily weather report.) Observant Muslim homes have prayer calendars and alarm clocks or preprogrammed computers that announce the prayer times, usually with recorded adan.

For all the emphasis on prayer, the rules governing it are surprisingly flexible. Prayers can be offered anywhere, on a spot that is clean. That is why you see Muslims praying in offices, factories, schools, bus stations, airports, hospitals, farm fields or in the rest areas along the highway. Muslims pray when it is time to pray, regardless of where they are. All they need to do is to figure out the direction of the holy city of Mecca in Saudi Arabia, turn toward it and begin the worship. During the 1980-88 Iran-Iraq war, I repeatedly witnessed the Iranian artillery corps on hilltops taking turns for their salah, with half the unit praying while the other half was busy blasting long-range guns.

Travelers have the choice of a shortened prayer, usually half:

When you go forth in the land, it is no sin for you to shorten the salah (4:101).

When ill, Muslims may pray lying in bed. If they find themselves in a confined space, they are freed from the requirements of standing and prostrating, and they pray in a sitting position. The next time you are on a plane and see a passenger seemingly lost to the world and unresponsive to others while moving her hands and lips, she is probably praying.

If, during the prayer, the mind wanders off and the believer forgets the sequence of the ritual, he or she simply adds one more prostration as a corrective. A mental lapse neither nullifies the prayer nor makes it any less pure. Humans make mistakes. It is the intent that counts.

If Muslims miss a prayer at the prescribed hour, they may add it to the next one. If they miss that as well, they may aggregate all the postponed ones and offer them at the end of the day. Each believer keeps his or her own tally. Parents may encourage — sometimes pester — their children with reminders; family members may exhort each other; and some Islamic states may even have moral police herding people into the mosques at prayer time. But, ultimately, the adherence to the daily prayers is a covenant between an individual and God.

The Role of the Mosque

Mosques may vary in size and architectural design, even in the style of minarets, but they are remarkably similar inside. There is space at the entrance to remove and store shoes; a separate area for washing (usually a pool in an open courtyard in tropical countries), a large, high-ceilinged prayer hall with low-hanging chandeliers, no furniture but rich carpets, decorative Qur'anic calligraphy on the walls and columns, and a niche up front for the *imam* (prayer leader). The imam may be on the mosque staff but is more likely a member of the congregation, chosen on the spot because he is an elder and is respected for his knowledge, piety and accurate recitation of the Qur'an. The consensus usually forms within seconds, a routine display of democracy.

The congregation lines up shoulder to shoulder, in straight rows, each line filled out fully before the next one begins to form. "*Allah-o-Akbar*, Allah is the most Great," the imam intones, lifts his hands to his ears and folds them on his chest. The congregation follows. As a pin-drop silence descends on the hall, he recites the first verses of the Qur'an:

> *In the name of Allah, the Beneficent and the Merciful*
> *All praises to Allah, the Lord of the Worlds*
> *The Beneficent and the Merciful*
> *Master of the Day of Judgment*
> *Thee we worship and Thee we beseech for help*
> *Guide us to the right path*
> *The path of those upon whom Thou has bestowed grace*
> *Not those upon whom Thine wrath has fallen*
> *Nor those who go astray* (1:1-7).

This is the most read chapter of the Qur'an. Being the prescribed opening of each of the seventeen parts of the five daily prayers, it is recited at least that many times by observant Muslims, who also recite it on countless other occasions because it encapsulates an essential element of their faith — total surrender to Allah.

The imam then reads a few lines from any other part of the holy book. He leads the congregation into half bowing, with hands on the knees, then goes down to prostrate with the forehead and palms touching the ground, and stands up again to repeat the cycle once, twice or thrice depending on the time of the day and, finally, sits with the feet tucked under the buttocks. It sounds difficult and can be for the uninitiated, but for those used to it, it is second nature.

The prayer over, usually in less than fifteen minutes, people greet each other. Many mingle and linger in the camaraderie that is the hallmark of such gatherings. A tea house, coffee house or restaurant is never too far from the mosque's courtyard. On foreign assignments, I find the mosque precincts to be the best locales for tasty and reasonably priced local cuisine, as well as for interviews to get a good read on public opinion.

Mosque-going Muslims get to know each other and the neighborhood, thereby enhancing social cohesion and developing strong communities, even in large urban centers.

The prayers are performed in the same manner across the world, except for minor variations. A Muslim can thus go to any place on earth, join others in prayer and feel at home, finding an instant bond with strangers. One of the first things a traveling Muslim usually does is to find out where the nearest mosque is.

Not every Muslim prays regularly or in the mosque. But enough do to have made the salah a powerful symbol, as noted admiringly by the late Pope John Paul: "From sincere Muslims, Christians can learn the courage of sincere prayer. They pray five times a day and no matter where they are, be it the railway station or the airport, they will do it, whereas many Christians are ashamed of making the sign of the Cross in a restaurant or pulling out a rosary on a train."

The Friday Prayer
Juma

On Fridays, the noon prayer (*juma*) must be said with others in a mosque, unless one finds oneself in a place with no other Muslims to form a congregation. In that case, the rule of flexibility reigns, and one reverts to the individual daily noon prayer. Women are exempted from the Friday prayer but are free to attend and, depending on cultural traditions, do.

Juma has higher attendance than the daily prayers. Friday is to Muslims what Sunday is to Christians, and Saturday is to Jews. In Muslim nations, Friday is usually a holiday, enabling the believers to enjoy the prayers and meet other Muslims at a leisurely pace. In Western nations, most employers permit their Muslim employees to adjust their lunch hour to take the needed hour or two. Increasingly, labor codes are being amended to give Muslim employees the same rights on Fridays as are conferred on Jewish workers for the Saturday Sabbath, with the employees making up the lost time.

The Festivals of Eid

Even bigger than juma are the gatherings for the Eid (rejoicing) festivals — the Eid al-fitr, at the end of the fasting month of Ramadan, and the Eid al-adha, two months and ten days later, which marks the day of Haj, the pilgrimage to Mecca.

Both Eid prayers — held after sunrise, usually around 8 or 9 AM — are generally offered in open grounds set aside for just this mass thanksgiving and community solidarity. In the West where Muslims are a minority, they rent big halls or stadiums for the two occasions.

Eid is the Muslim Christmas — a happy occasion for family and friends, and a time to exchange gifts.

An integral part of both the Eid and the weekly juma prayers is a sermon by the imam. The pulpit is a powerful platform from which to communicate with the people. That's how the 1979 Iranian revolution was brought about, with mosques serving as centers of mass mobilization. Dictatorial regimes, such as those in China, Russia and Egypt, control the contents of the sermons even more than they censor the media. Keeping mosques and the Eid prayer grounds under government control, they fire the priests who become critical. One of the ironies of the post-9/11 world is that many Western governments have also taken to surreptitiously monitoring the juma and the Eid sermons.

CHARITY
Zakat (to purify)

Almsgiving is so central to the faith that it is the third pillar of Islam, ahead of fasting and the pilgrimage to Mecca. *Pay the poor due* (2:83). *You shall not attain piety until you spend on others* (3:92). Several other verses encourage believers to be generous. Added Prophet Muhammad, "One who takes his fill while his neighbor starves is not a true believer." "An ignorant but generous man is dearer to Allah than a worshipper who is miserly."

Zakat is obligatory for those who can afford to give. And just about everyone can, within his or her means. The annual contribution, generally calculated privately and given voluntarily, is 2.5 percent of one's net worth. The aim is to redistribute wealth and establish a more just society—a precursor of the principle of progressive taxation.

The concept is made less abstract by the obligation to give first to kith and kin in need. "Those who look after their own relatives shall be doubly rewarded," said the Prophet.

After the family, the Qur'an tells the believers to show kindness to orphans and the destitute (2:83), and especially panhandlers. *Do not reject the beggar* (93:10). *In your wealth is a due share for the beggar and also to him who is too proud to beg* (51:19). When a particularly insensitive Conservative Party government in Ontario, Canada's largest province, banned panhandling in 2000, many Muslim Ontarians quietly doubled or tripled their giving.

Believers are enjoined to give without violating the dignity of the receiver. *Do not mar almsgiving with insults; those who do are like a rock covered with soil—one shower and it is bare. Such people will gain nothing for their deeds* (2:264).

Charity can be public, so as to encourage others, but it is preferably private. *To be charitable in public is good, but to give alms to the poor in private is better* (2:271). Said the Prophet, "Give so secretly that your left hand does not know what your right has given away."

Zakat sustains many poor Muslim nations, especially those also stricken by corruption. The work of helping the needy is invariably taken up by observant Muslims or Islamic grassroots organizations, which also provide a range of social services that the state often does not.

Another byproduct of zakat and the ethos of sharing is the legendary culture of hospitality among Muslims, most of whom live up to the Prophet's motto: "The food of one is enough for two, the food of two enough for four, and the food of four enough for eight." Travel through any Muslim land and you will find even the poorest of the poor ready to share their modest food and meager belongings with the visitor. On repeated visits through several Arab nations as well as Iran, Afghanistan, Pakistan, Bangladesh, Indonesia and Malaysia, I would stop to take a break or ask for directions, and within moments there would be tea, coffee and snacks or, depending on the time, full-fledged lunch or dinner — as well as an invitation to stay overnight as an honored guest. One of my fondest memories is of sitting in the shade of palm groves on blisteringly hot days and being offered dates and green Arab coffee flavored with cardamom.

FASTING
Sawm

Muslims fast from sunrise to sunset during the month of Ramadan, which may be 29 days or 30, depending on the sighting of the moon. The lunar year being only 354 days — 11 days shorter than the solar calendar — Ramadan rotates through the seasons. If one year it starts on December 1, the next year it will begin around November 19. Over a believer's lifetime, Ramadan will come in the hot and long days of summer as well as the cooler and shorter days of winter.

In the far north where the sun may never set or set too late, Muslims follow the timetable of the nearest city south of the Arctic Circle, or they divide the day into two twelve-hour halves, limiting their fast to a manageable time: *Allah wants to make things easy for you, not difficult* (2:185).

Muslims may also fast on other designated days of the year, though this is not compulsory. Among those days is the tenth of the lunar month of Muharram to commemorate the day the prophet's grandson, Hussain, was killed in battle. It is also the day Moses helped the Children of Israel escape persecution in Egypt. Prophet Muhammad urged Muslims to fast on that day in solidarity with the Jews.

Unlike the custom in some religions and cultures, the fast is total. One may not eat or drink, even water, or smoke, and must refrain from sex, from the time of pre-dawn breakfast to the end of the fast at dusk. Exempt are the very young, the old and the sick, along with pregnant women, nursing mothers, and those doing hard manual labor. Travelers are also exempt, but they must make up the missed days after Ramadan. Fasting becomes obligatory only upon puberty, but most children start earlier, swept up in the social euphoria and culinary delights that mark the breaking of the fast.

Fasting is sometimes referred to as the ultimate diet. But it is first and foremost an act of total submission to God. Only secondarily is it meant to make the believers experience hunger, so they may identify with the poor and the hungry. It is also designed to inculcate self-discipline, self-control, self-evaluation and patience. Muslims are regularly reminded that there would be no point to going hungry if they were to get crankier and ignore their obligations to be polite, considerate and kind to others at home, in the mosque, at work. *Deeni wa dunyavi*, the spiritual and the worldly.

Why does fasting take place during Ramadan? Because that was the month in which the Qur'an was revealed to the Prophet. Muslims try to read the entire scripture more than once during the month, reciting it in special night prayers. The last ten days of the month are considered the most blessed, and Muslims make an extra effort to stay awake and pray. Some take up residence in the mosque for a spiritual retreat of a few days. Every Ramadan, I am amazed to see so many Muslims going around with so little sleep, doing their regular jobs, fasting all day and spending a greater part of the night in prayers, operating on a spiritual high.

They are brought down to earth, however, as the lunar month draws to a close and the arguments begin over whether it really has ended. That depends on whether or not the sliver of the new moon has been sighted. That, in turn, will decide whether the community will celebrate the festival of Eid al-fitr the following day or the day after. Similar arguments afflict the timing of Eid al-adha, the festival that coincides with the annual pilgrimage of Haj. The confusion surrounding both may not matter much in Muslim nations where Eid is an automatic holiday, whenever it is proclaimed. But it does matter in nations where Muslims live as a minority and must arrange a day off work.

On the moon-sighting issue, the world of Islam is divided into two theological camps: those who say that science can surely tell when the new moon is to appear, and those who insist that it be sighted by the naked eye. The latter are further divided into those who say that one such sighting anywhere in the world is good enough, and those who insist that the moon be seen in each community. But what constitutes a community — a country, a city or a time zone? In a Muslim state, the government decides the issue. Whether people follow or not depends on how much Islamic legitimacy the state has, or how authoritarian it is, in which case citizens may have little choice. (In the first Ramadan after the toppling of Saddam Hussein, Iraqis had the first heated argument in decades about when fasting should begin.) Saudi Arabia, which must manage the traffic of millions of pilgrims, has adopted a combination of science and religion. Many around the world follow the Saudis but others don't.

The arguments, mostly good-natured, continue. So does the

confusion. But the centrality of Ramadan to Muslims remains solidly anchored.

PILGRIMAGE TO MECCA AND MEDINA
The Haj

Once in their lifetime, Muslim men and women go to Saudi Arabia for a pilgrimage to Mecca and environs, the birthplace of Muhammad and Islam. They also visit the city of Medina, 362 kilometers (225 miles) northwest, where the Prophet is buried.

Mecca is the site of the Ka'ba, the cubic structure toward which Muslims from around the world turn five times a day in prayer. Muslims believe it was first built by Prophet Adam and later by Prophet Ibrahim with his son Ismail. The Qur'an refers to the shrine as the Ancient House or the House of Ibrahim. *Undoubtedly, the first house of worship ever built for mankind is the one at Mecca* (3:96). *A pilgrimage to the house is a duty to Allah for those who can make the journey* (3:97).

Prophet Muhammad said that those coming to the Ka'ba are the "guests of God" and will have their sins forgiven and their prayers answered: "Those who perform the *Haj* will return from it as purified and sinless as they were on the day of their birth."

The Haj was promulgated in AD 628 when Muhammad was in Medina and the Ka'ba still under the control of his enemies. It was another three years before his followers could perform the first pilgrimage and yet another year before he did. Muslims have undertaken the sacred journey ever since, through wars, famines and natural calamities, swelling in numbers in every age of Islamic history — never more so than in the past twenty-five years.

Today, more than 2 million pilgrims, about 45 percent of them women, come every year from virtually every nation — a true global village. More would come except for the ceiling set by the Saudi government through a quota for most countries which, in turn, pull the names of eager applicants at random.

The Haj, which lasts a minimum of six days over five locations within 15 kilometers (9 miles), is the world's largest religious gathering. Muslims come because Allah told them to. Modernity, far from dampening their religiosity, has increased it.

The Saudis have spent $100 billion doubling the capacity of the holy mosques of Mecca and Medina — producing two architectural and artistic wonders in the process — as well as dramatically upgrading other Haj-related facilities. Saudi Arabia continues to enjoy enormous goodwill in the Muslim world for taking good care of Islam's holiest sites and ensuring the comfort of the pilgrims. This is one reason why the populist Western — principally American and British — criticism of Saudi Arabia finds so little resonance among Muslims, in spite of their own reservations about the undemocratic nature of the regime or its strict strain of Islam known as Wahhabism.

Just as the regular Friday congregation is an assembly of Muslims in a neighborhood and the two Eid celebrations are gatherings of Muslims in a city, the Haj is the grand congregation of Muslims of the world.

The Haj is incumbent on those who are reasonably healthy and can afford the trip — that is, those who have paid off their debts, whose livelihood would not be unduly affected by the undertaking, who have set aside enough for their dependants in their absence and who, ideally, have the consent of the elderly parents or sick members of the family reliant on their care. Muslims are prohibited from paying for the journey out of *haram* (unlawful) earnings, such as a windfall from gambling.

The Haj is not obligatory in times of war or natural disasters, when the safety of the pilgrims cannot be guaranteed.

In times past, pilgrims traversed overland routes or sailed weeks and months, especially from the Far East and the interior of Africa. Now they mostly fly into Jeddah, the port city on the Red Sea, landing at a swanky terminal designed for and utilized only in the Haj season. They travel by road to Mecca, 72 kilometers (45 miles) inland.

The pilgrims are swathed in the *ihram*, two seamless white pieces of cloth — one worn as a sarong from the navel down and the other draped over the left shoulder, leaving the right bare. With no jewelry, no perfume and no adornments, the bare-headed pilgrims stand as equals — the rich and the poor, the ruler and the ruled — regardless of color, ethnicity, nationality or any other attribute that might have defined their station in the worldly domain, which they have temporarily renounced to surrender themselves to God.

The women, so often shunned aside elsewhere, walk here as equals.

More than the dress, the ihram refers to the state of sanctity the pilgrims have entered: celibacy and non-violence — no hunting, no killing (not even hurting a pesky insect) and no aggressive behavior, such as losing temper. It is in this state of tranquility that they take up the devotional chant, the *talbiyah*, that echoes everywhere over the next few days:

Here I am, O Lord / Here I am at Thy service / Thou hath no partner / Here I am.

As they head toward the Great Mosque — the *Haram al-Sharif* (noble sanctuary), the locale of the Ka'ba — they are bursting with anticipation.

The Shrine of Shrines

As the pilgrims surge through one of the four main gates of the Great Mosque, they have their first breathtaking glimpse of the Ka'ba, squat in the center of a large open circular courtyard surrounded by the world's only circular mosque. The not-so-cubic object of their lifelong veneration and imagination is 15 by 10 meters (50 by 33 feet) at its base and 14 meters (45 feet) high, with a flat roof. It is hollow. The outside is draped in a black silk cloth with Qur'anic inscriptions hand-embroidered and embossed in golden and silver threads that shimmer in the sunshine and the permanently floodlit night.

The pilgrims, stunned into momentary silence, burst forth with the ecstatic cry of *Allah-o-Akbar*:

> *Allah is the greatest / There is no god but Allah / O Allah Glorify and enhance the majesty of this House, / and the reverence and piety it evokes from mankind.*

They rush to the east corner of the Ka'ba where a sacred black stone, a relic from the original structure, is set in a crevice. Every pilgrim wants to touch it, preferably kiss it, but rarely manages to, given the surging, jostling crowds. Gesturing a kiss, the pilgrims pronounce yet another supplication, and begin the most sacred rite, the *tawaf*, the counter-clockwise circling of the Ka'ba, reciting different prayers at different spots during different circuits. They run and walk. The old and the infirm, carried around in palanquins, raise their hands in supplication. The moving rings of humanity stop only for two purposes: when it is time for one of the five salahs or when a coffin has been brought for the rare honor of its funeral prayers being offered at the holiest of the holy grounds.

Facing the Ka'ba, the pilgrims gather in circles that get bigger and bigger (more than fifty in the courtyard), spilling over into the two floors and the rooftop of the Great Mosque and then out into the open piazzas — more than 800,000 people at the peak of the Haj. There is no sight quite like it in the world. The Great Mosque is twenty times larger than St. Peter's Basilica and five times larger than the world's largest soccer stadium, the Maracana, in Rio de Janeiro.

The prayer over, the pilgrims resume their circumambulation. They try to get close to the Ka'ba, and the luckier ones touch it or press themselves against it and pray — asking forgiveness for their sins, relief from their personal and family privations, and for an end to the suffering of Muslims in the trouble spots of the world. The supplicants may invoke each people by name — the Palestinians, the Iraqis, the Chechyns, the Kashmiris, the victims of tsunamis or earthquakes and whoever else may be in the throes of war, occupation, oppression and suffering — and beseech the Lord to help the besieged.

The pilgrims stop at a spot called the Place of Ibrahim, where Muslims believe he used to pray and where a rock that bears a miraculous print of his feet is encased in glass. They offer a special salah and proceed to drink from an adjacent well, called the *Zamzam*, which sustained Ibrahim's son Ismail as a child. So sacred is the water — the Prophet called it "food for the hungry and a cure for the sick" — that Muslims have been carrying samples of it back to their families and friends for hundreds of years, long before bottled spring water came into vogue.

Safa and Marwa
The pilgrims take a few steps east to the site where, 4,000 years ago, Ibrahim left his wife Hajera and their infant son Ismail, who was soon panting in the desert sun. Looking for water, Hajera

made a frantic dash between the hills of Safa and Marwa seven times until the Angel Gabriel pointed out the miracle of water springing up from the sand under the baby's heels. The Zamzam has flowed ever since.

Pilgrims re-enact Hajera's run between the two hills, which stand 500 meters (1,600 feet) apart, going back and forth seven times as their chants fill the canopied grand rectangular hall now covering the distance — an engineering feat far grander than roofing over entire street blocks for shopping malls. The sick and the old are wheeled up and down on a ramp. Atop each mount, pilgrims turn toward the Ka'ba and, eyes fixed on it, recite the Qur'anic line, *Indeed Safa and Marwa are among the signs of Allah* (2:158).

The visit to the Ka'ba and Safa and Marwa completes what is known as *Umrah*, the lesser pilgrimage, which can be performed at any time throughout the non-Haj months, as more than 2 million do every year. The Haj pilgrims, however, must press on with the third and fourth components of their journey.

On to Arafat

They begin moving out of Mecca onto a vast barren plain where they spend a minimum of three nights — usually four or more — at sacred sites.

One is Arafat, 15 kilometers (9 miles) away. Here in AD 632, the Prophet delivered his historic Haj sermon, outlining an Islamic charter of rights. By noon on the appointed day, the pilgrims converge, filling up every patch of the rocky valley as far as the eye can see, including every inch of a solitary granite hill called the Mount of Mercy, where the Prophet spoke. They are here for an afternoon of communal yet solitary prayer, during which they are usually oblivious to the burning heat, made only marginally more bearable by giant water sprinklers spraying a thin mist.

The valley resounds to the sounds of pilgrims in supplication, declaring repentance, seeking pardon, recommitting themselves to their faith and renewing their spirituality.

At sunset the multitudes begin their return journey and stop after 5 kilometers (3 miles) for an overnight sojourn at a place called Muzdalifah. The next morning they start moving to nearby Mina, armed with the pebbles they have collected along the way for their next mission.

Haj Facts[2]

Meals sold in the week of the Haj: 10 million
Meals served free: 2 million
Loaves of bread distributed: 40 million
Crowd control officers: 26,500
People treated as outpatients: 220,000
People treated in emergency: 48,000
Average natural deaths: 525

- Great Mosque at Mecca
  Area: 366,000 square meters (90 acres)
  People who can pray in the mosque and the piazza: 820,000
      Indoors: 486,000
      On the roof: 137,000
      Outside: 197,000
- Mosque of the Prophet at Medina
  Area: 108,000 square meters (27 acres)
  Height of its six new minarets: 104 meters (340 feet)
  Cooled water piped 7 kilometers (4.3 miles) to air-condition
      the mosque: 64,350 liters (17,000 US gallons) a minute
  Ceiling and wall fans: 1,292

Stoning the Satan

They pelt pebbles at three pillars that mark the three spots where Ismail stoned Satan, for tempting him to rebel when his father Ibrahim was leading him to the place of sacrifice. (Christians and Jews share this story, with a difference. In the Bible, Abraham was prepared to sacrifice not Ismail but the younger son Isaac, born of wife Sarah, and the locale was Jerusalem, not Mecca.)

The Haj pilgrims sacrifice a sheep, goat or a camel. Keeping a

People who can pray in and around it: 670,000
  Indoors: 150,000
  On the roof: 90,000
  Outside: 430,000

- Arafat
  Water-misting poles to cool down the pilgrims: 3,100
  Water used per day: 8.8 million liters (2.33 million US gallons)
- The Well of Zamzam
  Water bottled for Haj: 24 million liters (6.3 million US gallons)
  Number of bottles distributed free: 10 million
- Mina
  Area into which 2 million pilgrims are squeezed: 3.8 square kilometers (940 acres)
  Fire-proof Teflon tents for sleeping: 43,200
  Estimated number of pebbles pelted: 100 million
  Animals sacrificed: 1.1 million
  Estimated value of the meat donated for worldwide distribution: $100 million

symbolic portion for themselves, they donate most of the meat, which is frozen, packaged and shipped to the poorer parts of the world.

Male pilgrims have their heads shaved or merely trim a lock or two, as the women do. This marks the end of their state of ihram, and they change into their regular clothes, reverting to their colorful heterogeneity as quickly as they had embraced the homogeneity of the *ummah* (community).

The Haj is not over. The pilgrims must stay two more nights in Mina in meditation, sleeping in tents or on the open ground. During that period or following it, they return to the Ka'ba for one more round of circumambulations. The site and the ritual by now familiar, they are more relaxed, partly because they have fulfilled their lifelong dream.

They celebrate the Eid al-Adha, the festival of sacrifice. So do Muslims around the world, in congregational prayers in their communities, sacrificing an animal, donating most of the meat to food banks for use by Muslims and non-Muslims alike, and celebrating with family and friends.

The pilgrims in Mecca and Mina, physically exhausted but spiritually uplifted, start to depart — but not before their third and final visit to the Ka'ba for their farewell tawaf.

As of that moment, each male graduate of the Haj will be known as a Haji and each woman a Hajiyah, the honorific eliciting respect from fellow Muslims for the rest of their lives, regardless of where they go. It is a calling card exclusive to Muslims.

On to Holy Medina
Though not part of the Haj, pilgrims also visit the Masjid-e-Nabawi, the Mosque of the Prophet in Medina. They go there either prior to the Haj or immediately after it. Medina is where

the Prophet and his companions found refuge after fleeing persecution in his native Mecca. It was during his decade in Medina (622-32) that Muhammad consolidated the Muslim community, propagated Islam and controlled territory — the only prophet to have founded a state. *Deeni wa dunyavi*, the spiritual and the worldly.

His mosque stands at the spot where he ended his arduous journey of escape from Mecca. He insisted on paying for that land even though the owners offered it to him for free. He laid the first brick of the mosque and joined the volunteers in building it, carrying construction material on his back. He lived in an adjacent room, from where he would step into the mosque to lead the prayers and conduct the affairs of his nascent state.

It was in that modest abode that Muhammad died in the lap of his wife Ayesha, and that's where he was buried. The site has ever since been a magnet for millions who keep coming from the far corners of the earth — not just during the Haj season but year-round, every hour of every day and every night. Such has been the unremitting love of Muslims for their Muhammad.

HALAL AND HARAM
The Permitted and the Prohibited

In addition to the five basic pillars of Islam, Muslims follow a code of ethics that dictates what is *halal* (lawful) and *haram* (unlawful), as well as what falls in between — *makruh* (discouraged). Halal is most often associated with food and drink, similar to the Jewish kosher, but also encompasses other aspects of life.

> *O mankind! Eat of that which is lawful and wholesome in the earth* (2:168).

Forbidden unto you [for food] are carrion and blood and swine flesh, and that which hath been dedicated unto any other than Allah, and the strangled, and the dead through beating, and the dead through falling from a height, and that which hath been killed by [the goring of] horns, and the devoured of wild beasts, saving that which ye make lawful [by proper slaughter], and that which hath been immolated unto idols (5:3).

Halal Foods: Fish, legumes, nuts, grains, milk, vegetables, fruits and plants that do not cause intoxication. Also the meat of cows, goats, sheep, deer, moose and fowl (chickens, ducks, game birds, etc.) if slaughtered by a Muslim who says a prayer, like a rabbi conducting kosher slaughter. Muslims may eat kosher if halal meat is not easily available.

Haram Foods: Pork and its byproducts, carnivorous animals (those that tear their food apart with their claws, such as lions), almost all reptiles and insects, animals that died before being properly slaughtered, blood, and all alcoholic or intoxicating drinks.

Makruh Foods: Lobsters, crabs and most shellfish, excluding shrimps, which are permitted. Also discouraged is smoking, since it is addictive.

Haram Lifestyle: Gambling, including lotteries; all drugs that cause intoxication, alter sensory perception (hallucinogens) or affect one's ability to reason and make sound judgments; and paying and accepting interest.

Like the Bible, the Qur'an bans usury — interest on money. *Allah has cursed usury and blessed alms giving (2:276). That which you give in usury so that it may increase...will not increase with*

Allah (30:39). Muslims take the injunction seriously, even though not all Muslims follow the edict. But there is an increasing trend worldwide to patronize financial institutions that avoid interest altogether and charge a service fee instead, giving a return on investments in halal businesses (no stocks in liquor, tobacco, pornography, armaments or casinos).

The Dow Jones offers nearly fifty Islamic Indexes, which avoid the "sin stocks" and have consistently outperformed the

Islamic Etiquette

A Muslim invokes God at all times. A Muslim gets on a plane and before it takes off, says, *Bismillah-ir Rahman ar-Raheem* (I begin in the name of Allah). Many pronounce those words at the start of almost every activity — sipping water, eating food, turning the ignition key of a car, conducting a business transaction, signing a contract, writing a letter or sending an email. Muslims worldwide repeat that phrase countless billions of times a day.

A Muslim hears that President Bush has held a party for Muslims at the White House, and says, *Alhamdulillah* (Praise be to Allah).

A Muslim learns that Britain is pulling its troops out of Iraq and says, *Mashallah* (As Allah wills).

You make an appointment to meet a Muslim, and he or she says, *Inshallah* (If Allah wills).

You ask a Muslim about the terrorist mayhem, and he or she says, *Wallah-o-alam* (Only Allah knows).

These are routine Muslim responses, even for those who may not be very religious. It's their form of speech.

stock market by 5 percent. Muslims wanting to avoid the standard mortgages or car loans turn to co-ops in the US, Canada and Europe, which provide rent-to-own alternatives.[3] Major banks also offer Islamic banking. In 2005, Islamic-compliant investments, including mutual funds, totaled an estimated $665 billion (US) in more than 100 countries.[4]

THE QUR'AN

"What's the big deal?" wondered some Americans about the widespread backlash against the desecrations of the Qur'an in the detention center on Guantanamo Bay. Here's the answer. The Qur'an may be the most revered book in the world; it is certainly the most read and recited.

Muslims read from the Qur'an day and night. They read its opening chapter, the *Fatihah*, at least seventeen times a day in the five daily prayers. If only one-fifth of the 1.3 billion Muslims observe their daily canonical duties, those 260 million alone recite those verses more than 4.4 billion times a day. They follow up with readings from any of the Qur'an's 113 other chapters. They also routinely recite the Qur'an on both celebratory and sad occasions.

The opening line of every Qur'anic chapter — *In the name of Allah, the Beneficent and Merciful* — is on Muslim lips all the time.

Muslim homes invariably have a copy of the Qur'an and are also decorated with Qur'anic calligraphy. So are the domes, walls, columns, minarets and gates of mosques. Muslims may put Qur'anic stickers on their cars, at workplaces and in their wallets. They listen to the Qur'an in their cars. Airlines from Muslim nations usually dedicate a channel on their audio systems to Qur'anic recitations. Qur'anic tapes and CDs are a big business.

The Qur'an, which is in Arabic, is the only holy book that is memorized in its entirety. It is four-fifths the size of the New Testament. Undaunted, Muslims commit all its 86,430 words to memory. Those who do are called *huffaz* (plural of *hafiz*, one who remembers) and are held in high esteem. There are said to be 10 million of them.

What makes the achievement of the huffaz even more remarkable is that not all of them understand Arabic. In fact, the tradition of memorization is strongest in some non-Arabic nations, such as the Indian sub-continent. They commit it to heart because Prophet Muhammad told them to: "Retain and safeguard the Holy Qur'an in your memory."

Range of Beliefs

Like people of any faith, not all Muslims follow all the dictates of Islam. It is thought that only about a fifth go regularly to the mosque for the daily prayers, but it is difficult to know for sure. Muslims may pray individually or in small groups anywhere outside the mosques, as millions do.

It is also said that another fifth or more attend the juma, the Friday prayers.

An estimated two-thirds of Muslims turn up for the two Festivals of Eid.

There's no knowing how many observe the fast of the month of Ramadan, or how many give to charity.

But there's no doubting the trend toward greater Islamic observance. At the same time, non-practicing Muslims have no less a right to consider themselves Muslims, just as non-practicing Christians and Jews continue with their respective religious designations.

Memorizing the text takes an average of three to four years. Graduates may be prodigies as young as eight or nine. They are given the honor of leading adult congregations in the evening prayers at the mosque during the fasting month of Ramadan, when the entire Scripture is recited.

Another art form associated with the Qur'an is *qirat*, the melodious recitation of the verses by *qaris*, who have trained for years, like opera singers. In Malaysia, Pakistan, Egypt and Saudi Arabia, there is a strong tradition of qirat competitions, which attract large audiences. Top Qur'anic reciters are celebrities, with fans all over the world.

Such is the devotion of believing Muslims to the Qur'an that they are never far from it, physically or in spirit. To desecrate the Scripture, or to insult the Prophet to whom it was revealed, is to scar the soul of a Muslim.

Jews, Christians and Muslims all claim their holy books to have been the revealed words of God. Muslims also believe that the Qu'ran is the last of the revealed books, sent through Muhammad, who could neither read nor write.

The first revelation came in AD 610. He was forty years old and on a spiritual sojourn on a hill outside Mecca when he was thunderstruck by an overwhelming presence — that of Archangel Gabriel — ordering him to "Read." He said he did not know how. "Read." Again, he said he couldn't. "Read," commanded the Angel the third time, and proceeded to pronounce the first revelation:

> *Read in the name of your Lord who created*
> *He created man from a clot*
> *Read, your Lord is most honorable*
> *Who taught you to write with the pen* (96:1-4).

Muhammad had trouble believing he was the chosen one but

was convinced by family and friends that he was. The revelations, burnt into his heart, came over a period of twenty-two years, five months and fourteen days. A third came during his days in Mecca, and two-thirds during his decade in Medina (622-32).

To those who thought Muhammad was a soothsayer or a sorcerer or that he might have contrived the Scripture, Allah challenged the doubters:

> If they say, "he invented it," say, "then bring 10 surahs [chapters] like it of your devising" (11:13).

> And if you are in doubt as to that which We have revealed to Our servant, produce a chapter like it (2:23).

Muhammad challenged the best poets and storytellers of the day to match the breathtaking elegance and the broad sweep of the divine text. They couldn't.

Contemporary sensibilities are not immune to the magnetic force of the Qur'an. Stories abound of people entering Islam after listening to a recitation of it, or reading it in translation. Cat Stevens, the British folk singer, converted and became Yusuf Islam after he read a copy given to him by his brother. Cassius Clay also converted after reading the Qur'an and became Muhammad Ali.

The Prophet's followers memorized the Qur'an and inscribed it on stones, date palm branches, hides, the shoulder bones of camels and slates. After his death, the Qur'an was formally compiled under his successor Abu Bakr, the first caliph. There was a dispute over whether it had been transcribed accurately. So Umar, the second caliph, had it redone, employing a more vigorous methodology. Detractors still regurgitate that dispute and spice it with the assertion that if the Qur'an was God's words, why was it argued over? The answer, say the believers, is that the Qur'an was indeed God's, but the arguments were those of humans. The answer, from the perspective of modern democracies that guarantee freedom of religion, is that it is none of the state's business what any believers believe, as long as they are not breaking the law of the land.

The compilation of the Qur'an is not chronological; the chapters are not listed in the order revealed but by length, with the longest chapters at the start. There are 114 chapters in all.

Muhammad is mentioned in the Qur'an 5 times. Moses is mentioned 135 times, Abraham 67, Noah 43, Jesus 33, Joseph 27 and Adam 25. The only woman mentioned by name is Mary, mother of Jesus.

THE PROPHET

Sallallahu alaihi wassalam. That's what Muslims say every time they mention or hear Muhammad's name: "Peace be upon him" (PBUH).

While movies, television and other media proliferate in Muslim nations, tradition continues to forbid the depiction of the Prophet and his companions. The prohibition flows from the injunction against making images of the living God (Deuteronomy 4:16-19), which Muslims adopted. But there are enough detailed descriptions of him for Muslims to know him intimately. That's how the movie *Muhammad* (1977) was made, with him off-camera but his presence felt in almost every scene.

The Sermon That Changed the World

"There is no superiority for an Arab over a non-Arab and for a non-Arab over an Arab, nor for the white over the black, nor for the black over the white, except in piety." The Prophet Muhammad enunciated that message of equality, now the bedrock principle of democracies, back in AD 632.

He was delivering his now famous sermon during his only Haj pilgrimage to Mecca. He had come from Medina with 30,000 followers, insisting that the women come along. About 70,000 others had joined him along the way. After circumambulating the Ka'ba, the throng proceeded to the valley of Arafat, where he climbed the Mount of Mercy to deliver what amounted to his last will and testament.

"Hear me, O People, for I know not if ever I shall meet with you in this place after this year," he began, intending his words for more than those present. Instead of "O Muslims," he called out "O People" and "O Mankind" a total of eight times.

Emphasizing the plurality of humanity, Muhammad cited the Qur'an:

> O People, we created you from one male and one female, and made you into tribes and nations, so that you may know one another (49:13).

Muhammad proceeded to lay down a series of rules, which have since evolved into the basic principles of many civil societies today — the right to life, liberty and security of person (which have been guaranteed, for example, in Canada's Charter of Rights and Freedoms), and the right to private property (entrenched in the American constitution).

Speaking of the sanctity of human life and the need to end tribal savagery, Muhammad said, "Each man's life and possessions are sacrosanct. The blood feuds of pre-Islamic days are abolished. Every claim arising out of homicide is henceforth waived." To set a personal example, he announced that he was giving up one such outstanding claim of his own clan.

The Life of Muhammad

AD 570 Born in Mecca, Arabia.

595 Marries his boss, Khadijah, a rich widow.

610 Receives first revelation from God. The revelations continue for twenty-two years and constitute the Qur'an.

615 Muhammad's teachings infuriate locals who persecute him. He sends seventy to eighty followers to Ethiopia (Abyssinia), whose Christian ruler gives them refuge.

619 Khadijah dies, leaving four daughters but no sons (two died in infancy).

620 Muhammad, known for his integrity and leadership, is visited by a six-member delegation from the northern city of Yathrib, inviting him to move there and lead their five fractious tribes.

622 Migrates to Yathrib. The journey is called *Hijra* (the flight), from which the Muslim calendar is dated. So, AD 2006 is 1427 AH (After Hijrah). Yathrib is named Madinat al-Nabi (City of the Prophet), shortened to Medina.

624 First battle against the Meccans; 313 Muslims defeat 1,000 Meccans.

625 Second battle against the Meccans; 1,000 Muslims are routed by 3,000 Meccans, who mutilate Muslim corpses. Muhammad is injured but salvages an honorable retreat.

627 Third battle against the Meccans; the Meccan army of

He followed with an economic manifesto — the obligation to pay off debts and stand by financial guarantees, and the duty to avoid usury and other types of economic exploitation: "Your capital and your property are sacred and inviolate and yours to keep. You will neither inflict nor suffer injustice. All debts must be repaid, all borrowed property must be returned, all gifts must be

10,000 lays siege to Medina but is unable to enter because of a ditch dug around the city. The Meccans run out of provisions in two weeks and leave.

628 Muhammad goes to Mecca with 1,600 pilgrims to visit the Ka'ba. He is not allowed to enter but negotiates a ten-year truce.

630 After the Meccans break the truce by murdering a tribe allied to Muhammad, he returns with an army of 10,000. The Meccans submit without battle and Muhammad announces a general amnesty: "May Allah pardon you. Go in peace." He cleanses the Ka'ba of idols but does not force locals to convert to Islam, although many do.

631 Muhammad receives delegations from all over Arabia; they swear allegiance to him. He sends a delegation to Palestine and concludes a treaty with the Christians there.

632 Muhammad goes to Mecca for his farewell Haj and gives his last sermon. Two months later, on June 8, he dies in Medina, at age sixty-two, leaving several wives he had married after Khadijah's death, one daughter and no sons.

Today There are more people in the world called Muhammad than by any other name.

reciprocated, and all financial losses compensated by the guarantors. All interest and usurious dues accruing from the pre-Islamic age also stand waived." Again, leading by personal example, he said he would pay back all the interest charged by a money-lending uncle.

"O People, you have certain rights over your women and your women have certain rights over you... It is for them not to commit acts of impropriety, which if they do, you are authorized to separate them from your beds and chastise them, but not harmfully... My dictum to you is that you treat women well and be kind to them for they are your partners." The words were revolutionary for the times.

Muhammad's next admonition, regarding the treatment of slaves, was similarly pioneering: "Your slaves are your brethren. See to it that you feed them with such food as you eat yourselves and clothe them with the clothes you yourselves wear. If a black slave is appointed your emir [leader], listen to him and obey him."

After reminding the believers to adhere to the teachings of the Qur'an, including giving charity regularly and performing the Haj, he called for Muslim solidarity: "Muslims constitute one brotherhood. Every Muslim is a brother unto other Muslims. Therefore, the property of one is unlawful to the other unless given willingly. Do not be unjust to one another."

He warned against religious extremism, something that many imams and other Muslims today would do well to heed: "Be moderate in religious matters, for excesses caused the destruction of earlier communities."

He was almost finished.

"O People, have I faithfully delivered unto you my message?" he asked. "O God, yea!" replied the multitude. The

Prophet raised his forefinger and said, "O Lord, bear witness."

The rest of the day was spent in meditation. At sunset, the Prophet mounted his camel, followed by the rest. As a commotion broke out, he cried, "Gently, gently! In quietness of soul! And let the strong among you have a care for the weak."

The Wisdom of Muhammad

The sayings of Muhammad are among the treasures of mankind.
— Mahatma Gandhi

Family
One who cuts off family ties does not enter the Garden of Paradise.

Women
God enjoins you to treat women well.
Do not forbid your wife to go to the mosque.

The Young
He is not one of us who does not treat the young with compassion.
Let the younger ones salute the elderly, let the one walking salute those sitting, and let those small in number salute those larger in number.

Neighbors
He is not a believer if his neighbor does not feel safe from his treachery.
Never scoff at a neighbor's gift, even if it is sheep's hooves.

Manners
The most odious of men are those who quarrel.
Do not snoop.
God hath not made it lawful for you to enter the houses of others without their permission.
Control your anger.
The exercise of religious duties will not atone for an abusive tongue.
No father has given his child anything better than good manners.

Visiting the Sick
Visit the sick and comfort them.

Charity
Give ungrudgingly; do not hold back, lest God holds back from you.
One's wealth does not diminish with charity.

Moderation

Let each of you pray to the extent of your energy; then sit down when you are tired.

Be moderate in religion.

Modesty

Do not lavish praise on me like the Christians lavish praise on the son of Mary. I am only a slave. Call me God's slave and messenger.

Non-Muslims

All prophets are brothers, with different mothers but one religion.

I am close to Jesus, in this world and the Hereafter.

Do not consider me better than Moses.

When the bier of anyone passes you, whether Jew, Christian or Muslim, rise to your feet.

Once Muhammad got up when a bier went by and he was told: "This is the bier of a Jew." He responded: "So what, did it not have a soul?"

Travel

Travel is torment, interfering with sleeping, eating and drinking. So when you have concluded your business, hasten to your family.

Keeping Good Company

Beware of hanging around in the streets. The people said: "That's the only place we have to sit and chat." In that case, give the street its rights. They asked: "What are the rights of the street?" He said: "Those on it should lower their gaze, refrain from causing trouble to others, return people's greetings, and enjoin good and forbid evil."

Animals

Fear God in how you treat animals.

Suicide

Let none of you wish for death because of a loss or harm that has befallen you.

Muslim Sects / Spiritual Divisions

Sunnis and Shiites

About 87 percent of all Muslims (1.05 billion) are Sunnis — those who follow the *sunnah* (sayings and deeds) of the Prophet Muhammad.

The remaining 13 percent (170 million) are Shiites (also known as Shia or Shiat Ali, the party of Ali, the fourth caliph of Islam, whom they follow). Shiites constitute the religious majority in Iran, Iraq, Bahrain, Yemen and Azerbaijan, and they are the largest religious group in Lebanon.

Sufis

Sufis are Muslim mystics who practice Sufism. Unlike the division between the majority Sunnis and the minority Shiites, which is based on a dispute over who should have succeeded the Prophet Muhammad, the distinction between Sufis and non-Sufi Muslims is "a vertical division." Sufis may be Sunnis or Shiites.

The word sufi comes from *suf* (wool). It refers to the coarse garments worn by early Muslims as protest against the silks and satins of the sultans and caliphs. The dissidents' complaint was that Muslims were becoming too worldly and less spiritual. "Love the pitcher less and the water more," they said. Develop your inner core to "experience God."[5]

Going beyond the rituals of religion, these mystics try to achieve God consciousness through *dhikr* (remembrance) of God. They repeat some of Allah's ninety-nine names or sing poetry to music or dance themselves into a trance, turning right to left or going around in circles, as do the famous Sufis known as the Whirling Dervishes.

Early Sufis clustered around masters and formed circles that developed into Sufi orders.

Muslims are of two minds about Sufis. That's because some Sufis take liberties with, or profess no allegiance to, the basics of the faith. Others create a cult of sainthood, leading to a veneration of, and pilgrimages to, mausoleums of the saints. Yet others believe in magic and superstition. Such aberrations raise eyebrows.

Sufis played an important role in spreading Islam, especially in Russia, the Indian Subcontinent and the Far East.

Rumi, the Sufi Poet

Rumi is the best-selling poet in the US. A mystic, Jalal al-Din Rumi (1207-1273) was born in Iran, but his family moved to Turkey during the Mongol invasion. He grew up to be a Sufi *mawlana* (teacher), but fell under the spell of another, Shams al-Din, and became his student. After Shams died, or was murdered, Rumi became desolate and took to writing poetry.

His enormous output includes *Mathnawi* (Epic), containing six books of 25,000 rhyming couplets, as well as 2,500 mystical odes and at least 1,600 quatrains. Rumi would recite the verses whenever or wherever they occurred to him — "dancing, in the bath, standing, sitting, walking, by day or by night."[6] Today he is considered the greatest mystic poet of Persia and possibly in all of Islam.

Offshoots of Islam

Alevis: 6 million to 20 million, mostly in Turkey and in Germany. De-emphasize the daily prayer, fasting and the pilgrimage of Haj.

Bahais: 7 million. Syed Mirza Ali, a nineteenth-century Iranian, claimed to be a new manifestation of God and took on the title of "the Bab" (the Gate). Members of the Bahai faith are followers of Baha'Ullah, a disciple of the Bab. The Bahai headquarters are in Haifa, Israel, near the spot where Baha'Ullah died.

Nusayris/Alawites: 1 million, mostly in Syria. Also called Alawites (not to be confused with the Alevis).

Druze: 750,000 to 1 million, mostly in Lebanon, Syria and Israel. They are an offshoot of Shi'ites.

Ahmadis: 10 million. Named after Mirza Ghulam Ahmad (1835-1908), who claimed to be the Islamic Mahdi, the Messiah and the last avatar of the Hindu God Vishnu. Ahmadis are also known as the Ahmaddiya or as Qadiyanis, after the town of Qadiyan in Punjab.

Chapter 4
Women

IMAGE AND REALITY

The West has a fixed image of the Muslim woman. She is a second-class citizen.

She is forced to wear a veil — or worse, a head-to-toe tent-like cloak — when going out, if she is allowed to go out at all. She may be subjected to genital mutilation. If she has premarital sex or an affair during marriage, she may be publicly stoned to death or murdered in "honor killings." She may not marry a non-Muslim — an edict that does not apply to men, who can wed Christians and Jews and take four wives. She may not have an abortion. She will inherit less property than a man. Her testimony is worth only half that of a man.

Western stereotypes of Islam have been around for centuries. "The treatment of women provided Europeans with an excuse to declare the inferiority of Muslims and their religion, and also justification for Europe's imperialist and colonialist policies and practices," writes Guity Nashat, professor of history at the University of Illinois.[1] A telling example was that of Lord Cromer, British consul in Egypt toward the end of the nineteenth century, who said the "degradation of Muslim women" proved the "backwardness of Islam," even while he was a founding member of the Men's League for Opposing Women's Suffrage in England.[2]

But Muslim women are neither as badly off as they come

across in the Western media, nor do they enjoy the idealized protected lives that some Muslims would have us believe. Some Muslims talk of how Islam liberated women, which it did in Arabia in the seventh century, yet they are silent on the second-class status of women in most Muslim societies today. Let us set aside the polemics of both sides and take stock.

While men are still leading the US and most of Europe and Africa (Germany elected its first woman chancellor in 2005, the same year that the African continent got its first woman president, in Liberia), and Japan remains in a state of national anxiety over the prospect of a woman ascending to the Chrysanthemum Throne because both sons of Emperor Akihito have produced only daughters, Muslims have readily entrusted their affairs to women.

Indonesia, the largest Muslim nation, has had a woman leader. So has the second largest, Pakistan. And the third largest, Bangladesh. And the fourth largest, Turkey.

Indonesian president Megawati Sukarnoputri, Turkish prime minister Tansu Ciller and Bangladesh prime minister Sheikha Hasina served one term each. Pakistan's Benazir Bhutto and Bangladesh's Khaleda Zia were elected prime minister not once but twice.

In India — whose Muslim minority of about 145 million is, in fact, nearly as large as or larger than the Muslim majorities in Pakistan (158 million) and Bangladesh (120 million) — Muslim women routinely hold cabinet posts and other high-ranking jobs.

In Iran, which has the world's sixth-largest Muslim population and where the hijab is mandatory, there has been a woman vice-president, Masoumeh Ebtekar, who in 1998 condemned the Taliban's treatment of women long before the rest of the world got around to it. The Iranian parliament has also had a higher proportion of women than the US Senate.

In Pakistan, the proportion of female members in the federal parliament is 21.3 percent — well above the world average of 11.6 percent; in Indonesia, it is 11.3 percent.[3]

In Malaysia, the head of the central bank is a woman. So are the attorney general and the solicitor general and the head of the space agency.

Bahrain's Haya Rashed al-Khalifa is, as of September 2006, the first woman president of the United Nations General Assembly since 1969.

Pakistan's Arfa Karim Randhawa is one of the world's youngest Microsoft Certified Professionals. On meeting Bill Gates, the ten-year-old asked why it was that even in 2005, about 75 percent of Microsoft's professional employees were men.

Across the Muslim world, female enrolment in schools and universities is at record levels, as is the number of women teachers and professors. The Arab world is showing the fastest improvement in female education of any region. Arab women's literacy rates have tripled since 1970. Their primary and secondary enrolment rates have doubled. In Jordan, the literacy rate for women is 84 percent, and in Iran it is 80 percent. In Lebanon, girls outnumber boys in both primary and secondary schools. In Saudi Arabia, more women are graduating from universities than men. In Iran, women outnumber men in post-secondary institutions, and a third of faculty members are women.

Yet amid much progress, patriarchy is alive and well.

The Taliban were toppled from power in Afghanistan, thanks to the United States. Yet Taliban-like rules prevail in Saudi Arabia, thanks in large measure to the US, its biggest patron and protector, which turns a blind eye to the suffocating restrictions on Saudi women. They must be covered head to toe in black before venturing out in public, which they may do only if escorted by a male member of the family. So strict has the enforcement of the dress code been that in 2001, fifteen girls at a school in Mecca died in a fire when the *mutawwah* (religious police) reportedly did not let them out of the burning building because they were insufficiently covered.

Saudi women are, as of this writing, not allowed to drive. On November 6, 1991, when forty-seven of them drove in protest in Riyadh for fifteen minutes, they were denounced as morally lax. Many were fired from their jobs. It was only after much lobbying that they were quietly allowed to return to work.

Not all the Saudi restrictions are Islamic. The taboo against women drivers, for example, is not *haram* (forbidden), but it is not permitted, in deference to tradition.

In Kuwait, the other close US ally in the oil-rich region, women didn't get to vote until 2006.

In the Arab world — twenty-two nations totaling 280 million people — gender equity remains elusive. According to the 2003 United Nations Arab Human Development Report, half of Arab women are illiterate, representing two-thirds of the 65 million Arabs who cannot read or write. Arab women have a lower life expectancy than the world average, due partly to high maternal mortality rates. The report praises Jordan and Egypt for ensuring the Islamic right of women to initiate divorce. But there are few other bright spots.

Despite their progress, Iranian women cannot shake the hands of men in public. They cannot leave the country without the permission of the male head of the family. They face legal discrimination in marriage, divorce and child custody. Of the 195 articles of the 1981 constitution, 107 deal with sexual activities, affecting women far more than men.

In Africa, the application of sharia in Nigeria has had a disproportionate impact on women. In the Muslim-majority north, where some states have adopted Islamic law, women are targeted for moral transgressions and are sometimes condemned to lashes or, in isolated cases, to death by stoning. Such measures run counter not only to the Nigerian constitution but to Islamic jurisprudence.

Sadly, misogynist interpretations of Islam are not restricted to Nigeria or Afghanistan and Pakistan. In many Muslim lands, fidelity to faith is measured in delivering the harshest judgments on women, especially poor ones. Few errant princes are ever whipped.

THE QUR'AN AND WOMEN

The Qur'an does not single out Eve for blame but depicts Adam and Eve as equally responsible for sin. Eve is not the temptress. She is not responsible for the fall of humanity. The Biblical assertion that Eve was created from Adam's rib also has no echo in the Qur'an.

The Qur'an "explicitly forbids depicting God as a figurative father," writes Asma Barlas, leading American Islamic feminist. "Nor does it treat fathers or fatherhood as sacred. It does not say that males embody divine attributes and that women are by nature weak."[4] In that sense, the Qur'anic sensibility is post-feminist.

"Nowhere does the Qur'an state that one gender is superior to the other," notes Canadian Islamic scholar Jamal Badawi of St. Mary's University, Halifax, a prolific writer on contemporary Islamic issues. "Men and women have the same religious and moral duties and responsibilities."[5]

In the Qur'an, Allah often addresses both men and women,

ordains similar religious duties and makes it clear that women have the same claim to Paradise as men:

For Muslim men and for Muslim women
For men who believe and for women who believe
For men who obey and for women who obey
For men who speak the truth and for women who speak the
    truth
For men who persevere in righteousness and for women who
    persevere in righteousness
For men who are humble and for women who are humble
For men who give charity and for women who give charity
For men who fast and for women who fast
For men who guard their modesty and for women who
    guard their modesty
For men who praise God and for women who praise God
For all of them, God has prepared forgiveness and a vast
    reward (33.35).

Wives are garments for you
    while you are garments for them (2:187).

The believing men and the believing women
    they are guardians of each other (9:71).

Whoever does right, whether male or female…
    We shall pay them recompense (16.97).

I shall not let the deeds of anyone go to waste, male or
    female; both are the same in this respect (3:195).

Those who give alms, be they men or women
    shall receive a rich recompense. (57:18).

Allah has promised to the believing men and the believing women
Gardens with rivers flowing under them…
and fine dwellings in the Garden of Eden (9:72).

All such Qur'anic declarations were revolutionary, and still are. Why, then, are Muslims arguing over smaller inheritances for wives, women's testimony being worth half that of men, honor killings, female circumcision, the stoning of women and polygamy?

HALF INHERITANCE

To men belongs a share of that which the parents and near-relatives leave behind
To women belongs a share of that which the parents and near-relatives leave behind (4:7).

Islam sees the male as the head of the family, and the woman primarily as the preserver of the family, the central unit of social stability — as do Christianity, Judaism and Hinduism.

In a Muslim marriage, the woman's consent is essential, her right to refuse absolute. Parents or others who ignore her wishes are breaking Islamic law.

Women have complete economic independence, before and after marriage. A woman can keep property in her name (a right not granted women in France until 1938).

A Muslim woman can do what she wishes with her wealth and possessions, without the consent of her husband. Unlike her husband, she is not required to contribute financially to the household, even if she has an independent income from a job or a business. Her earnings are hers to keep. Regardless of her income and personal assets, she has no legal obligation to even contribute to her own upkeep. This is why she inherits half of what males do, while keeping all her own accumulated property and wealth, over which the man has no legal right.

The man is responsible for providing inheritance not just to his wife but to the extended family, including daughters, sisters and grandmothers. In fact, the mother and the sisters are better off under Islamic laws, since they are ensured an inheritance from both sons and brothers.

Daughters cannot be deprived of their portion of an inheritance, as they can be under some Canadian, American and European jurisdictions. Under Islamic law, they cannot be disinherited even through a written will.

The Western discourse on the plight of Muslim women is almost exclusively about wives, not the other women of the family. As hard as it may be to accept, the Western feminist legal cosmos is far more limited than Islam's.

HALF TESTIMONY

The Qur'anic reference to discounting women's testimony comes as part of a consumer advisory that loan agreements are best put in writing and vouched by witnesses:

> Write it down between you with fairness... and call in to witness from among your men two witnesses; but if there are not two men, then one man and two women (2:282).

But in another reference to the rules governing witnesses, the Qur'an makes no distinction between the testimonies of men and women:

> Let him testify four times... Let her testify four times (24:6-8).

Still, there is no question that in many parts of the Muslim world, women's testimony is given only half the weight. Even those committed to restoring the rights of women don't quite seem to know how to proceed. "This is one of the truly problematic areas that we face," Muhammad Zahid, an Islamic scholar and a volunteer imam in Toronto, told me in 2005. "The *ulemah* (scholars) need to address it."

DOMESTIC VIOLENCE

Men are the maintainers of women… The good women are, therefore, obedient, guarding the unseen as Allah has guarded; and (as to) those on whose part you fear desertion, admonish them, and leave them alone in the sleeping places and beat them; then if they obey you, do not seek a way against them (4:34).

Beat them? For centuries, Muslims have been arguing over whether that's the right interpretation of the Arabic words in question, *fadhri bouhon*. Other interpretations have been "turn away from them," "scourge them" or "tap them." But in popular usage, "beat them" has beaten those other variations.

Many scholars argue that the instruction is symbolic rather than literal, and that it does not sanction violence against wives. They point out that the Qur'an also says, *O you who believe! It is not lawful for you to take women against their will, nor to hinder them (from re-marrying).… Treat them kindly* (4:19).

Prophet Muhammad never beat his wives, of course. And he campaigned vigorously against the tribal custom of violence against women. Most scholars have declared domestic violence to be religiously forbidden. "Anyone who says the Qur'an allows you to beat your wife is telling an egregious lie. It is *haram* to be violent against your wife or children," Hamza Yusuf, imam and charismatic American convert to Islam based in California, said in an interview in 2005.

This does not mean that there is no spousal abuse among Muslims. There clearly is. Muslims are no better than other people. But are they worse?

In its campaign against violence against women, Amnesty International points out that it takes place in every society, across class, race, culture and religion. In Europe, for example, "domestic violence is the major cause of death and disability for women aged 16 to 44, and accounts for more death and ill-health than cancer or traffic accidents."[6] Even in Sweden, which pioneered gender equity laws, the National Council for Crime Prevention has reported a near doubling of violence against women.[7] The United Nations reports widespread violence against women in sub-Saharan Africa: one in three Nigerian women report that they have been physically abused by a male partner; in South Africa, a male partner kills a girlfriend or spouse every six hours.[8] And 31 percent of American women report having been victims of violence by a male partner.

Yet sweeping and disproportionate denunciations of Muslim men continue, as do the denials of Muslim men about the problems that Muslim women do continue to face.

HONOR KILLINGS

The despicable and dishonorable practice of killing women for sexual misconduct has nothing to do with Islam, even though it does take place in Muslim societies such as Pakistan, Turkey, Jordan and the Israeli-occupied Territories. But this cultural practice is not restricted to Muslims. One of the most brutal murders in 2005 was that of Faten Habash of Ramallah, a Christian Palestinian, reportedly bludgeoned to death by her father because she wanted to marry a Muslim.[9] In British Columbia in 2005, a Sikh was convicted of killing his daughter who was pursuing an interracial relationship.[10]

Yet the impulse to link the crime with Islam seems irresistible. Take the horrible case of Hatin Surucu, a Kurdish German shot dead at a Berlin bus stop in 2005 for abandoning her husband from Turkey and trying to start an independent life. Her brother was implicated in the crime. No sooner had the story hit the headlines than fingers were pointed at Turks and Muslims in Germany. As Riem Spielhaus of Humboldt University pointed out in a 2005 interview in Berlin, "Some guy who happens to be a Turkish Kurd does that and, suddenly, all Turks are 'honor killers' and all Muslims are 'honor killers.'"

But as long as some Muslims are implicated in this crime, it is incumbent on all to expose it and help root it out. The public awareness campaign launched in Jordan in 2001 and in Turkey in 2005 were therefore welcome, all the more so because, in the case of Jordan, members of the royal family took the lead, and, in the case of Turkey, clerics appeared in television ads to denounce honor killings as "un-Islamic."[11]

GENITAL MUTILATION

The Qur'an, like the Bible, makes no mention of female genital mutilation, though some early Islamic scholars accepted it as an African tradition. The tragedy is that this pre-Islamic barbarity endures, in varying degrees, in north and central Africa (where not just Muslims but Christians and animists practice it) and some Muslim clerics continue to justify it in religious terms. Muslims in the rest of the Middle East, Asia and the Far East are generally unaware of it.

There is nothing in Islam encouraging the mutilation of

female genitalia. That's why many Islamic scholars joined Western feminists in the 1990s to campaign against genital mutilation. Almost all African states have since banned the practice. Canada and others have made it a criminal offence following reports of clandestine operations in pockets of Somali and Ethiopian communities. At the First Islamic Ministerial Conference on the Child in Rabat, Morocco, in 2005, ministers and religious leaders from almost fifty nations called genital mutilation un-Islamic and pledged measures to crack down on the practice.[12]

ADULTERY AND STONING

Contrary to popular belief, the Qur'an does not prescribe stoning for adultery, or for any other sin. It does stipulate harsh punishment, for both men and women: *As for the adulterer and the adulteress, scourge each of them with a hundred stripes* (24:2). *As for the two who are guilty of indecency from among you, punish them both* (4:16).

But no one can be convicted without the testimony of four witnesses: *As for those who are guilty of indecency from among your women, call to witness against them four from among you* (4:15). Four credible witnesses would have had to have a ringside view of penile penetration to have the accused convicted. The chance of that in an Islamic society is less than zero. Yet this legal requirement of testimony by four reliable witnesses is rarely adhered to. Perversely, this rule is turned against the woman in the case of rape, by requiring that *she* produce four witnesses that she indeed was raped.

The Qur'an also warns against false accusation: *And those who accuse free women but do not bring four witnesses, scourge them with eighty stripes, and never admit any evidence from them* (24:4). This protection for women is rarely provided by the sharia court or, in many cases, even by the parallel civilian courts, so patriarchal is the system in many Muslim nations.

POLYGAMY

Notwithstanding Western assumptions, monogamy is the norm among Muslims. An overwhelming majority of Muslim males have only one wife. While neither the Old nor the New Testament abolished polygamy, the Qur'an regularized the pre-Islamic practice after the Muslims' second war in AD 625, in which 10 percent of the 1,000 warriors were killed, leaving many widows and orphans.

Encouraging the faithful to be fair to those two groups, the Qur'an says,

> *Give to the orphans their property, and do not substitute*
> *worthless [things] for their good ones, and do not devour*
> *their property; this is surely a great crime.*
> *And if you fear that you cannot act equitably toward*
> *orphans, then marry such women... two or three or four;*
> *but if you fear that you will not do justice [between*
> *them], then marry only one* (4:2-3).

However, later in the same chapter, the believers are told, *You have it not in your power to do justice between the wives, even though you may wish it* (4.129). Thus the conundrum: Men may marry more than once if they can treat the wives equally, which they cannot. "This is essentially an exhortation in favor of monogamy," writes Wiebke Walther in *Women in Islam*.[13]

Some Muslim states, or states with large Muslim minorities, seeing polygamy as discriminatory to women or as a violation of the Qur'anic principle of equal treatment of all wives, have enacted restrictions on the practice—either banning it altogether, as in Tunisia, or banning it for civil servants, as in India, or placing conditions on it, such as requiring the man to obtain the first wife's written permission.

In the West, the issue comes up most in France, where it is alleged that since France offers subsidies for housing and children, Muslims multiply benefits through polygamy. But, tellingly, there is no data, in the absence of which bigots, including politicians and journalists, can be as irresponsible as they like. Agence France Press news agency, for example, released a story in May 2005 headlined "Polygamy flourishing in France," and reported "the existence of an estimated 30,000 families in which there is more than one wife." It cited no source. Deutsche Welle, Germany's international broadcaster, inflated the number, again with no reference to a database, or even an attribution, claiming that "between 150,000 and 400,000 people live in polygamous households in France."[14] That's quite a range, from 30,000 to 400,000!

Still, if even 30,000 residents of France are violating the 1993 French ban on polygamy, the real issue surely is why the French police are not enforcing the law and charging the polygamists. That is what authorities in the state of Utah and the province of British Columbia are, at last, proposing to do with the polygamists among a splinter sect of Mormons known as the Fundamentalist Church of Jesus Christ of Latter Day Saints.

The only sane policy is for the state to enforce the law and the citizens to obey it, including Muslims. For them it would, in fact, be an Islamic obligation, since they are expected to follow the law of the land where they live, unless it prohibits them from practicing the basics of their faith. Polygamy is not one of the five essentials of Islam. Therefore, anyone desirous of having more than one wife is free to leave for another jurisdiction.

DIVORCE AND CHILD CUSTODY

Unlike the Catholic aversion to divorce and annulment, and unlike the very restrictive divorce laws prevalent in most Western nations until recent years, Islam from its beginning allowed divorce on grounds of incompatibility, cruelty, injustice, adultery and insanity — about the same grounds that contemporary divorce laws cite for dissolving a marriage.

The Qur'an permits divorce but recommends reconciliation:

> *If you fear a breach between the two, then appoint an arbitrator from his people and an arbitrator from her people; if they both desire agreement, Allah will effect harmony between them* (4:35).

Added Muhammad, "Of all things permitted by God, He dislikes divorce the most." But if there is to be one, the Qur'anic guiding principles are clear:

> *Hold together on equitable terms, or separate with kindness* (2:229).
> *And when you have divorced women...release them in a just manner* (2:231).

The injunctions, directed at men, are clear. In matters of divorce, be civil, get third-party arbitration and don't keep the separated wife dangling by withholding divorce — prescient principles applicable to many contemporary males, Muslims and non-Muslims alike.

In Islam, marriage is not a sacrament. It is a civil contract, akin to a prenuptial agreement, pioneered 1,400 years before Jacqueline Kennedy and Aristotle Onassis popularized it. The *mehr* (often wrongly translated as "dowry" instead of the more appropriate "gift") that the Muslim man promises the woman is a legal stipulation designed as a deterrent against a hasty dissolution of marriage — by him. He must pay before walking out. The only way he can legally avoid the payment is if she waives the mehr; if she chooses not to, the divorce is not complete. The protection is designed for her.

In the case of marriage breakdown, children under seven are to be in the care of the mother. After that, boys have a choice between staying with either parent, while the daughter must stay with the mother. At puberty, both have a choice, though some religious schools of thought prefer that daughters continue to stay with the mother.

Muslim women have the right to initiate divorce without the consent of the estranged husband. But in practice, a woman is rarely allowed to proceed by the male-dominated religious and civilian courts. Abandoned women are thus left in limbo. Their plight is the same as that of Orthodox Jewish women, whose estranged husbands deny them the *get* (the Jewish divorce), without which women cannot remarry.

Not all Muslim men follow the Islamic rules, of course. Violations vary from region to region, culture to culture. But often they are camouflaged under the rubric of Islam which, in turn, further feeds the Western penchant for equating cultural practices with Islam.

MARRYING NON-MUSLIMS

Do not marry the idolatresses until they believe; a believing maid is better than an idolatress woman, even though you may admire her; and do not give [believing women] in marriage to idolaters until they believe; a believing servant is better than an idolater, even though you may admire him (2:221).

Neither are these [believing women] lawful for them [the unbelievers], nor are those men lawful for them (60:10).

The injunctions apply to both men and women. However, in practice, Muslim men have been allowed to marry Christians and Jews. Muslim women have not.

Two arguments have been advanced to rationalize this discrimination. The first claims that the children of male Muslims are considered Muslims by default and should be raised as Muslims. And since the husband is considered the head of the family and is expected to set the direction and the values of the family, it is more permissible for him to marry a non-Muslim than for a woman. The second holds that while Muslims accept the divine origins of Judaism and Christianity, Jews and Christians do not believe in the prophecy and the message of Muhammad. Therefore, a Muslim woman cannot live with someone who does not believe in the message of Muhammad.

Islamic feminists, especially in Malaysia and Indonesia, contend that one rule should apply to both men and women — a position that is slowly gaining ground.

THE QUR'AN AND THE HIJAB

A majority of Muslim women do not wear the hijab. This is true not just of those living in the West but across the world. This reality is at odds with the media image of women walking around in tent-like garments.

Not all those who reject the hijab are anti-religious. A handful are. But the rest are not transgressing their faith by not wearing the hijab. Their action is not comparable to that of Catholic women who refuse to obey the dictates of the Pope on contraception and abortion. Non-hijabi women are merely following liberal interpretations of the Qur'an. Never once does the Qur'an instruct women to cover their faces. In fact, during the pilgrimage to the holy city of Mecca, women are required to uncover their faces and hands. So where does the hijab come from?

The scripture only urges modesty for both women and men:

> *Say to the believing men that they cast down their looks*
> *and guard their private parts....*
> *And say to the believing women that they cast down their*
> *looks and guard their private parts and do not display*
> *their ornaments except what appears thereof and let*
> *them wear their head-coverings over their bosoms*
> *(24:30-31).*

Allah is clearly asking more of women in this context. But scholars are divided over what is meant by "ornaments" or "adornments," the other word used in translations. Is that a reference to a woman's natural beauty or to her jewelry or other fashion accoutrements? And what is meant by "what appears thereof"? No one is sure. No one ever can be.

There is also a debate over another pertinent Qur'anic verse:

> *O Prophet! Say to your wives and your daughters and the*
> *women of the believers that they let down upon them their*
> *over-garments; this will be more proper, that they may be*
> *known, and thus will not be molested (33:59).*

The conservative interpretation — mostly by men, of course — has been that women must cover themselves from head to toe. But even under such a reading, the results have varied from culture to culture — from the Taliban's all-enveloping burqa, with only slits for eyes, to the chador wrapped like a shawl on the upper part of the body and head, leaving the face exposed, as in Iran or parts of Pakistan and India.

Some other verses in the Qur'an have an impact on this debate as well:

> *O wives of the Prophet! You are not like any other women...*
> *Stay in your houses and do not display your finery like in the*
> *time of ignorance* [the pre-Islamic period] (33:32-33).

> *O you who believe! Do not enter the houses of the Prophet*
> *unless permission is given to you... And when you ask of*
> *them [his wives] any goods, ask of them from behind a cur-*
> *tain; this is purer for your hearts and their hearts* (33:53).

The edicts are clearly addressed to the household of the Prophet during whose lifetime women outside his household did not wear the veil. Yet some theologians have held that the rule applies to all Muslim women, the argument being that emulating the Prophet's family can only be good.

Gender separation is sometimes cultural, and not confined to Muslims. In India, some Hindu women have been as much segregated as Muslim women. As I approached adulthood, I was no longer allowed in the women's quarters of the houses of some of my Hindu friends. And when women of those Hindu households ventured out, they, too, were veiled or had the curtains of their cars or horse-drawn *tongas* fully drawn. In other regions, sexual segregation is still a function of middle-class values. Poor Muslim women, especially in rural areas, have always gone out unveiled with their men to scratch out a livelihood.

MUHAMMAD AND WOMEN

Muhammad respected women — a radical notion for his era — and he broke many sexual and social taboos of his time. He shared housework — from sweeping the floor to undertaking other menial tasks. He spoke out against domestic violence. "Is it not a shame that one of you beats his wife?" "The best among you is the best to his wife." "Only a wicked man humiliates his wife." "Paradise lies under the feet of your mother."

He urged women to educate themselves. He was confident enough not to let his own illiteracy hold back the women of his household or those outside it. "The search for knowledge is a duty for every Muslim man and woman," he said, and he invited women to attend his lectures, which they often did, and participate in discussions.

Muhammad discouraged the then prevailing practice of female genital mutilation. He banned female infanticide, the practice of burying newborn girls alive. He banned the custom of a son inheriting his stepmother after the father's death. He condemned the practice of parents selling daughters at puberty.

He exhibited little or no prudery about sex. "I love to adorn myself for the woman, just as I love her to adorn herself for me." "I am interested in three things: perfume, woman and prayer." "Marriage is half the religion."

Writes Moroccan feminist Fatima Mernissi: "Muhammad was a chief of state who publicly acknowledged the importance of affection and sex in life...He was not an asexual man completely consumed by the quest for power...His military and religious activities did not ever cause him to devalue his private life or to relegate it to the background."[15]

His first wife, Khadijah, was said to be forty years old when he was only twenty-five. She was wealthy, he was poor. She was, in fact, his boss. A trader, she had employed him to conduct her business. She was not only impressed with his industriousness and honesty but was also captivated by him. It was she who proposed marriage through an intermediary. When he responded with a visit, she told him, "I love thee for thy kinship with me; and I love thee for thy trustworthiness and for the beauty of thy character and the truth of thy speech."[16] He accepted and moved into the bride's house. They lived happily for almost twenty-five years, during which time he stayed monogamous — itself a break from the norm, since men routinely used to have more than one wife. It was after her death that he married a dozen times.

As per a Qur'anic recommendation, he married widows, eight in all. Two had been widowed thrice and another two twice, including Khadijah. Two of his wives were divorcees. Most were women in their thirties and late forties. Only his child-bride, Ayesha, was a virgin. There are arguments over how young she really was when betrothed to him and when they married. Accounts vary, from age nine to thirteen, the normal age of marriage at that time, and even today for millions of teenage brides in the Indian Subcontinent and sub-Saharan Africa.

Muhammad often married outside his tribe, mostly to consolidate his expanding domain — a much-used modus operandi of many rulers. Two of his wives were Jews and one a Coptic Christian. But fostering political alliances was not his sole motive. He was a human being who was attracted to women. All of his relationships were open. He had no closet affairs that came to light later. No secret mistresses or children born outside of marriage materialized at his funeral, as in the case of both French president François Mitterand and former Canadian prime minister Pierre Trudeau. Nor was Muhammad the first prophet or patriarch to have practiced polygamy — Abraham, Jacob, Moses, Hosea, Saul, David and Solomon kept multiple wives or concubines.

Yet Westerners remain curiously obsessed with Muhammad's sex life. Even as they become voracious consumers of sexually explicit TV shows and movies, as well as of biographies of sports heroes boasting of hundreds of one-night stands, many North Americans and Europeans continue to be vituperatively prurient about Muhammad.

SHARIA AND WOMEN

Islam gave women the right to inheritance and divorce centuries before the West did. It gave them the right to own and manage property. Early Muslim women maintained separate accounts, initiated marriage, dictated prenuptial contracts and kept their maiden names. They participated in public debates and made a seminal contribution to religious texts and traditions. Women often assisted and sometimes fought in wars with the Prophet and, later, in the bloody succession feuds that followed his death. Women poets and singers performed at public gatherings and competed with men.

However, as Islam spread far and wide and Muslims got away from the pioneering spirit of reform, several factors undermined the status of women.

In the period after Muhammad, sharia proved unfriendly to women. Developed over a period of 200 years, the Islamic law was based mainly on the Qur'an and the *hadith* (the sayings and deeds of the Prophet). But the collection of sayings did not begin until well after his death, in a chaotic period of civil war. "Forging hadith became a flourishing industry; different interests used to twist the sayings of the Prophet for their own use," writes Asghar

Ali Engineer, a Muslim scholar based in Mumbai.[17] At one time, there were 700,000 hadith in circulation.

For example, there is still much argument over three ostensible sayings of the Prophet: "A people who hand their leadership over to a woman will not succeed." "I do not leave after me any cause for fear, except that of women to men." "I was shown the Paradise and the majority of the people I saw there were the poor; I was shown the Hell, and the majority there were women." Some scholars have said that the first saying was a general statement that allowed for exceptions, as seen even during the Prophet's time when women did play leading roles. The second was deemed a general warning about illicit sexual relations. And the third was circumscribed by an explanation offered by the Prophet himself when confronted by a woman angered by his pronouncement; he told her he was referring only to those women who unfairly blamed their husbands. Islamic feminists, however, question the very authenticity of those sayings. Fatima Mernissi has traced in historic detail the unreliability of the attributions. American academic Aisha Bewley suggests that the Prophet's saying about not entrusting power to a woman was forged twenty-six years after his death.[18] In any case, all three sayings are clearly out of character with all of Muhammad's words and deeds.

After Muslims conquered the Iranian Empire, parts of the Greek Byzantine Empire and Hindu India, they were ruling over populations whose women were restricted to household activities and child rearing. Even as the locals embraced Islam, they did not give up all their social practices. And local jurists writing new Islamic laws began "interpreting the Qur'an in a manner that reflected their older cultural value system," writes Guity Nashat.[19]

Women were relegated to a subordinate role by the end of the tenth century. By the thirteenth century, polygamy and the seclusion and segregation of the sexes had become common. "The position of woman sank to the low level we find in the *Arabian Nights*," wrote Philip Hitti in his classic *History of the Arabs*. "There the woman is represented as the personification of cunning and intrigue, and as the repository of all base sentiments and unworthy thoughts."[20]

Women were veiled and relegated to the *zenanah* (women's quarters) or, in the case of the debauched rich, to the harem. They were shut out of the public realm, including the mosque, which is why they took to visiting the shrines of Sufis and mystics where they were welcome, and still are. Travel through any Muslim country where Sufi shrines are allowed — they are not in the more puritanical states — and you will find almost as many women as men pilgrims.

The restrictions on women, instead of relaxing with the passage of time, kept getting worse. The separation of the world of men and women was complete well before the European colonization of Muslim lands. This is one area where Muslims cannot blame the West for their woes. In fact, some of the more regressive policies toward women have emerged in the past two or three decades, with the growth of fundamentalism among Muslims. But fundamentalists are being challenged by a new generation of Islamic feminists.

ISLAMIC FEMINISM

There are two main discourses on Muslim women — one largely but not exclusively among Muslims and the other, more dominant, in the Western media. "To the Muslim ear, [Western] feminist discourse smacks of colonial imperialism," writes Waleed Aly, a Melbourne lawyer active in the Islamic Council of Victoria in Australia. "Feminism and imperialism seemed to have some kind of undisclosed memorandum of understanding. Feminists only defend a woman's right to choose when she chooses to renounce Islamic norms but not when she chooses to adopt them."[21]

As for the debate among Muslims, a growing number of women and men do recognize the patriarchy that prevails in the Muslim world, and they are battling it. It is difficult to pigeon-hole them, since feminism can mean different things to different people. They include secular-minded Muslim feminists living in the West as well as in Muslim lands, who tend to think along the same lines as Western feminists. Among them are Muslim women estranged from Islam for intellectual or personal reasons, whose bitter anti-Islamic tirades are lapped up by the media.

Then there are Islamic feminists — believers who are fighting for women's rights within the fold of Islam. They get little or no press, either in the West or in Muslim lands, even though they are growing in influence and may hold the key to eventual progress. Asma Barlas draws the distinction between Islamic feminists and secular Muslim feminists this way: Most secular Muslim feminists "don't believe in a God, nor do they find it meaningful to engage the Qur'an or even to read it."[22] They are generally distrusted by the believers.

Islamic feminists argue that gender inequity does not emanate from Islam. They, like their Christian and Jewish counterparts, are rereading their scriptures "to demonstrate that the original texts are less misogynistic than they appear, and that alternative feminist readings have equal validity," writes British author Malise Ruthven.[23]

Islamic feminists — hijabis and non-hijabis alike — want to reinstate for women the central role they played during the

Prophetic period and in the years immediately following. This is not to say that women want to go back 1,400 years, but rather that they want their liberation within the framework of Islam. The sentiment was captured in the famous slogan of Afghan women directed at the Americans after the toppling of the Taliban: "Bring us your democracy, not your bikinis."

The same thought has been expressed by American human rights advocate Amy Gutman of Princeton University, who has said: "Oppressed women typically want their rights as individuals to be secured within their own culture, not at the expense of exile from their culture or the destruction of what they and others take to be valuable about their culture."

Some feminists may use the religious framework as a matter of tactics. The best way — sometimes the only way — to make headway with most Muslims is to speak the lingua franca of Islam. But "for most Muslim women, rejecting religion is not an option," writes Zainah Anwar of the Malaysian group Sisters in Islam. "We are believers, and as believers we want to find liberation, truth and justice from within our faith."[24] When her group condemned the Malaysian moral police squads for raiding nightclubs and private homes, it invoked the Qur'anic command against invading people's privacy: *Enter not houses other than your own, until you've asked permission and saluted those in them* (24:27).

Similarly, Indonesian Islamic feminist Musdah Mulia, director of research at the federal ministry of religious affairs, takes on the conservatives on their own religious turf. In a 2005 interview with me, calling for a ban on polygamy, she invoked the Qur'anic principle that men might be incapable of "justice between wives." Another Indonesian feminist, Lily Munir, author of *The Koranic Spirit of Gender Equity*, argues that it is not the scripture but social conventions that have dictated the mistreatment of women. This line of reasoning started in the 1980s and gained momentum in the 1990s, especially in Iran and Saudi Arabia.

In Egypt, Suad Salih, dean of the Women's College at Al-Azhar, the Islamic academy in Cairo, argues that nothing in the religion bars women from being appointed *qadis* (judges). Three were appointed in January 2005 in Egypt, joining those already at work in Syria and Turkey.

The feminist movement is not confined to women. Indonesian writer Husein Muhammad Nuruzzaman bases his arguments for gender equity on classical texts. "Many rules run counter to the moral message of Islam," he told me in 2005. American academic Khaled Abou El-Fadl, professor of law at UCLA and author of *Speaking in God's Name: Islamic Law, Authority and Women*, relies on authentic sources to make his points. So does Tariq Ramadan, Europe's leading Muslim intellectual.

There is no consensus among Muslims on issues such as abortion or homosexuality or women priests, just as there isn't in other religions. While women have led all-female congregations since the time of the Prophet and do so now in Iran and parts of China and South Africa, Muslim orthodoxy, like that of Catholic and some Protestant churches, resists women leading mixed congregations.

In fact, a full-fledged debate is underway on all aspects of women's position in Islam. Grassroots organizations dedicated to women's advocacy work are springing up in most Muslim nations as well as in Europe and North America. Many carry on spirited debates in magazines, weeklies and on the Web.

There is even an argument over the main argument — whether going backward is the best way forward. Fatima Mernissi says, echoing a broadly held sentiment, "the journey back in time is essential."[25]

The hope of resurrecting the past has not stopped women from acting in the present. A new breed of Islamist women is emerging across Europe, as exemplified by the hijab-wearing Hanife Karakus of Limoges, the first woman to lead one of France's twenty-five regional Islamic councils. Mosque-going women in North America, angry at being assigned the worst spaces for praying and for being relegated to kitchen duties, have made their views known. A poll by the Islamic Society of North America, the umbrella group of many mosques, found gender equity at the top of the respondents' concerns. "People felt that women weren't well treated and were excluded from decision-making," said Ingrid Mattson, vice-president of the society.[26] The complaint is not confined to women. Khaled El-Fadl says there is little or nothing in Islamic jurisprudence decreeing that women must pray in a separate room. After all, at the two holy mosques of Mecca and Medina, women pray in the same area as men, perform all the same rites as men, shoulder to shoulder with men. In the early period of Islam, women joined men at the mosque not only to pray but to debate the issues of the day.

There have also been complaints about the religious and cultural conservatism of the imams and the leaders of many mosques and Muslim organizations in Canada and the United States. Much of this, however, is largely an immigrant phenomenon not confined to Muslims. North America, with its rich history of immigration, has seen over the past 200 years that the first generation of immigrants, regardless of their origins, tended to turn to religion to keep their identity. They became more religious than they were "back home," and those most active in the churches tended to be more conservative. Immigrants often had no choice but to import priests from the "old country" — priests who generally did not speak English well, could not offer appropriate religious guidance to suit the changing social and cultural milieu, and who ended up alienating the younger parishioners. It took the next generation to produce local priests and a new leadership to reshape the church and its institutions to their more liberal and ecumenical liking. This has been the experience of virtually every immigrant community — the Poles, the Ukrainians, the Italians and others. It is an evolutionary process.

Islamic feminism is clearly "a global phenomenon," says Margot Badran of the Center for Muslim-Christian Understanding at Georgetown University, Washington, DC. "It is not the product of the East or the West. It transcends both. Who's afraid of Islamic feminism? Quite a few people. They include non-Muslims who fear Islam, and Muslims who fear feminism. They make strange bedfellows."[27]

Echoing the growing feminist sentiment, Nobel laureate Shirin Ebadi of Iran told me in 2005, "God created us all as equals. By fighting for equal status, we are doing what God wants us to do." Indonesian Islamic feminist Musdah Mulia framed the thought this way in her conversation with me: "Most Islamic laws affecting women are man-made. They didn't come as a fax from heaven."

Islamic feminism represents the dawn of a new era. It presents, for the first time in recent memory, a comprehensive and coherent basis for the emancipation of Muslim women. In doing so, it offers an alternative to Western secular feminism, which never did find too many converts among Muslims.

Muslims must acknowledge that "women are the targets of the most serious violations of human rights in Muslim societies," notes Riffat Hassan, professor of religious studies and humanities at the University of Louisville, Kentucky.[28] For their part, Western democracies should know that they cannot dictate the terms of the debate about the liberation of Muslim women. In fact, the harder the West — the US in particular — tries to control it, by continuing the current hostile discourse against Muslims and by embracing Muslim thinkers in its own image, the more skepticism and anger it will face, thereby adding to the already dangerous level of mutual hostility.

Chapter 5
Jihad and Terrorism

Does the Qur'an condone terrorism? This is the kind of question no one asks of his or her own religion; we save it for others.

— Professor John Esposito,
Georgetown University[1]

Every Muslim must do *jihad* (struggle). Most do. In the literal meaning of that word, they strive in the path of God by observing the five essentials of Islam and trying to be good human beings.

The Prophet Muhammad, upon returning from one war, said, "We have come from the smaller jihad to the greater jihad." Asked what he meant, he replied, "The jihad against oneself."

The word jihad strikes fear in the West, where it is understood solely in terms of war, but it is a more benign word for most Muslims. To them, the first jihad is the struggle against the ego. Then there's the jihad against the devil. There's also the jihad of the tongue to spread the word of Islam. There's the jihad of charity. There's the jihad of the pen to spread knowledge. These are all individual jihads.

Muslims are also sometimes urged to undertake similarly peaceful but collective jihads for the most mundane matters, such as the jihad for cleanliness, once declared by the Egyptian government; the jihad for literacy, initiated by the Tunisian government; the jihad against corruption in government, periodically proclaimed in Pakistan with little or no success; the jihad for water conservation, routinely called for in tropical countries, and so on.

"Nowadays, jihad is often used without any religious connotation, more or less equivalent to the English word, crusade — 'a crusade against drugs,'" writes Rudolph Peters, professor at the University of Amsterdam. "If used in the religious context, the adjective 'Islamic' or 'holy' is added to jihad."[2]

But in the West, where jihad is a highly charged term, especially since 9/11, we have had two parallel discourses. Those looking to discredit Islam insist that it is an inherently violent religion. "Look, it says right here in the Qur'an," they say. Osama bin Laden and other terrorists quote those same Qur'anic passages to justify terrorism. But most Muslims and many non-Muslims say Islam is a religion of peace, and they resent that both Islamophobes and militant Muslims are twisting its meaning to suit their disparate agendas.

Falling somewhere in the middle is the Western media narrative on holy war. The American media, in particular, have played hot and cold on the issue. They were highly critical when Iranians rallied under the Islamic banner for the 1979 revolution that toppled the pro-American dictator, the Shah. But during the US-backed 1980-89 holy war against the Soviet occupation of Afghanistan, the media glorified the 35,000 Mujahideen (those waging jihad) who had been recruited from forty-three Muslim countries and paid for by the Central Intelligence Agency, and whom President Ronald Reagan had called the moral equivalent of America's founding fathers. Dan Rather, CBS-TV news anchor, proudly posed on the Afghan frontier wearing the local costume of long shirt and pantaloons, as if he had joined the jihad himself.

The media adopted a more neutral tone during Saddam Hussein's 1980-88 war on Iran, which he called a jihad and which the United States supported. The media became hostile when Israel and America were targeted — by the Hezbollah during the 1982-2000 Israeli occupation of Lebanon, by some Palestinians during the second intifadah, by al Qaeda on 9/11 and by various groups since in occupied Iraq and elsewhere.

Holy war is good when it suits the West but evil when it doesn't.

THE QUR'AN AND JIHAD

What does the Qur'an say about jihad? It says a lot. It does so in the so-called sword verses, of which there are about a dozen. Both the critics of Islam and the likes of bin Laden quote these, selectively and out of context.

Take the injunction, *Slay them wherever you come upon them.* It is part of a passage that emphasizes self-defense when attacked:

> *Fight in the way of God with those who fight you, but do not initiate hostilities.*
> *God loves not the aggressors.*
> *And slay them wherever you come upon them, and expel them from where they expelled you; for persecution is worse than slaying* (2:190-92).

Another "sword" verse, *Take them and slay them wherever you come on them,* is part of an injunction revealed at a time when Muslims were being persecuted in Arabia:

> *If they leave you alone and do not fight you and offer you*

peace, then Allah allows you no way against them. [But] if
they withdraw not from you nor offer you peace, then take
them and slay them wherever you come on them (4:90).

Another oft-cited verse, *Fight the leaders of unbelief,* has a pre-
ceding qualifier, so that the full line reads:

If they break their pledges after their covenant and assail your
*   religion, then fight the leaders of unbelief* (9:12).

Similarly, when critics trot out the line, *Leave is given to those*
who fight, they rarely quote the entire injunction:

Leave is given to those who fight, because they have been
*   wronged... [and] expelled from their homes unjustly*
*   only for saying, "Our Lord is God."*
Had it not been for God repelling some men by means of
*   others, cloisters, churches, oratories and mosques, wherein*
*   God's name is oft mentioned, would surely have been*
*   pulled down* (22:39-40).

There are two elements here — one of defensive jihad to
counter the religious persecution that Muhammad and his followers were then facing, and the other of concern for the religious
freedom of all believers, not just Muslims.

As for the Prophet being a warrior, the concept is not unique
to Islam. What of Joshua, David and Solomon? Plus,
Muhammad "only fought those who fought him, and his fighting had no other aims than repelling repression, warding off
rebellion and aggression, and putting an end to persecution due
to religion," wrote the late Mahmud Shaltut, a former rector of
the famed Al-Azhar Islamic academy in Cairo.[3]

Islamic tradition holds that the verses relating to wars and
fighting were overtaken by the peace that followed between

Muslims and non-Muslims. Hence the later Qur'anic exhortations to avoid war altogether, to limit warfare, to honor treaties and, if attacked, to respond only proportionately, to protect civilian non-combatants and not to mutilate the dead:

Fight them [only] until there is no persecution (8:39).

If your enemy inclines toward peace, then you, too, should seek peace and put your trust in God (8:61).

Warfare is an awesome evil (2:217).

The overall Qur'anic message is clear, said Shaltut: "There are only three reasons for fighting: repelling aggression, protecting Islam and defending religious freedom."[4]

Can Muslims undertake a jihad to spread Islam by killing infidels? Arguments on this flow from this Qur'anic line:

When the sacred months have passed, slay the idolaters wherever you find them, and take them and confine them, and prepare to ambush them (9:5).

However, this, too, is qualified by what follows:

But if they repent and establish worship and pay the zakat [charity], *then let them go their way, for God is forgiving and kind* (9:5).

Such verses were "directed at a certain people, who had broken their pledges and hindered and assailed the propagation of Islam," Shaltut wrote. "The verses do not say that the quality of being an unbeliever constitutes sufficient reason for fighting."[5]

The Qur'an lays down two clear guidelines for Muslim relations with non-Muslims — one of brotherhood with Christians and Jews, and the other of religious freedom and pluralism for all humanity:

> *Dispute not with the People of the Book [Jews and Christians] save in the most courteous manner, and say: "We believe in what has been sent down to us and what has been sent down to you; Our God and your God is one, and to Him we surrender"* (29:46).

> *If God had willed, He would have made you one nation* (5:48).

> *Had thy Lord willed, He would have made mankind one nation; but they continue in their differences* (11.118).

"There is not a single trace of any idea of conversion by force," said Shaltut. "The Qur'an states clearly and distinctly that faith produced by force is without value and that he who yields to force and changes his faith loses his honor."

This takes us to the popular belief that Islam was spread by the sword. Islam did win converts as the Muslim armies conquered vast swaths of land in the first hundred years after the Prophet's death. But what is forgotten or ignored is that a majority of people ruled by Muslims remained non-Muslims. Furthermore, Islam expanded into China, Indonesia, Malaysia, the Philippines and sub-Saharan Africa primarily through traders and the non-violent Sufi saints. What is also forgotten is that it was Christians, not Muslims, who expelled the Jews from Spain in the fifteenth century, and later the Muslims: "Every Muslim was driven from Spain, put to the sword or forced to convert whereas the seat of the Eastern Orthodox Church remains in Istanbul [Turkey] to this day."[6]

Is jihad the responsibility of the state or an individual? Most

Muslim scholars have said that only the state can initiate holy war and that, too, only with the consent of the religious authority in the land. But people like bin Laden believe that when Muslim states fail to fight off foreign/non-Muslim aggression against Muslims — such as in Chechnya, Iraq or Palestine — then it is the duty of every Muslim to take up arms against the enemy. This view is shared by some but not by an overwhelming majority of Muslim scholars or ordinary Muslims. If it were, there would have been a mass movement to join bin Laden's various jihads, rather than the few thousand who follow him.

Can jihad be launched against fellow Muslims? Yes, say those rebelling against a Muslim state, because the ruler is unjust or cavorting with a non-Muslim enemy. This, again, is the view of bin Laden and others, which is why he and his supporters have launched terrorist attacks against his homeland, Saudi Arabia. To them, the Saudi regime is too pro-American.

Overall, there is broad consensus that terrorism is *not* jihad but a perversion of the holy texts. These are "deviant ideas that are used as justification for terrorism," declared the 2005 summit of the Islamic Conference.[7]

As John Esposito says, "Islam, like all world religions, neither supports nor requires illegitimate violence. Like all scriptures, Islamic sacred texts must be read within the social and political contexts in which they were revealed. It is not surprising that the Qur'an, like the Hebrew Scriptures or Old Testament, has verses that address fighting and the conduct of war."[8]

SUICIDE BOMBING

In the Second World War, Japanese kamikaze pilots rammed their planes into Allied ships, and Soviet pilots crashed into bridges in Germany. Imperial Japan held up those suicide missions as the ultimate military valor, and the Allies saw the Soviet pilots as anti-Nazi heroes. During the Vietnam War, Buddhist monks committed self-immolations to protest the American military presence and, in Sri Lanka, to highlight Sinhalese demands. Their suicides were not used as a weapon to kill others, but they shared the trait of self-sacrifice with those willing to die for their cause.

In contemporary times, those who have made the most extensive use of suicide bombings, to the end of 2004, are the Sri Lankan Tamil Tigers, who are Hindus. Their best-known use of the human weapon was in 1991, when a female suicide bomber assassinated Indian prime minister Rajiv Gandhi, who had sent Indian troops to help out the Sri Lankan government contain the Tamil insurgency.

Islam forbids suicide — in the same way other religions do — since only God has the right to take life. Both the Qur'an and the Prophet Muhammad prohibited suicide.

Top religious authorities in Saudi Arabia, Egypt and elsewhere have condemned suicide bombings in the strongest terms. Within hours of 9/11, leading Muslim scholars expressed their outrage and called the act un-Islamic. "But very little or none of that was reported by the Western media; what was reported instead was that some Muslims believed in the conspiracy theory that 9/11 was either a Jewish plot or that the American government itself was in on it," Malaysian human rights activist Chandra Muzaffar told me in 2005 in Kuala Lumpur, echoing a widely held Muslim view.

Similarly, in the wake of the subway bombings in London, Muslim scholars were emphatic in their denunciations. Declared Sheikh Sayed Mohammed Tantawi, head of Al-Azhar in Cairo, "Those responsible for the London attacks are criminals who do not represent Islam."

Muslim organizations in the West have also spoken out. "Islam condemns terrorism," read a sign at a Florida turnpike, sponsored by the Council on American-Islamic Relations, as part of its campaign, "Not in the name of Islam."

However, some Muslim theologians and political leaders, while condemning suicide for personal reasons, have justified suicide bombing to resist the Israeli occupation. Among them was Sheikh Ahmed Yasin — the religious leader and founder of the militant Islamic group Hamas — who was later assassinated by Israel, along with several others. Posters in the Israeli Occupied Territories read, "Israel has nuclear bombs, we have human bombs." The same logic is used by Tamil Tigers. "Of course, we use suicide bombers; as a revolutionary organization, we have limited resources," a Tiger spokesman has said.[9]

Robert Pape of the University of Chicago analyzed every suicide bomber attack between 1980 and early 2004 — a total of 462 incidents — and compiled his results in his book, *Dying to Win*. He concluded that Islamic fundamentalism "has very little to do with suicide terrorism, which is a response to occupation. From Lebanon to Sri Lanka to Chechnya to Kashmir to the West Bank, every major suicide terrorist campaign — over 95 percent of all the incidents — has had its central objective to compel the democratic state to withdraw."[10]

The suicide bombings usually stop once the occupying forces have withdrawn: "Once Israel withdrew from Lebanon, the suicide strikers did not follow Israel to Tel Aviv." He then points out that "the longer the American forces stay on the ground in the Arabian Peninsula, the greater the risk of the next 9/11, whether that is a suicide attack, a nuclear attack or a biological attack."[11]

JIHAD AND MARTYRDOM

Huston Smith, America's foremost authority on world religions, notes that both Islam and Christianity glorify those who die in holy wars and promise them salvation.[12] Indeed, most religions and cultures celebrate their martyrs. Tamil suicide martyrs in the Tamil-held areas of Sri Lanka and Palestinian martyrs in the Occupied Territories are publicly hailed.

The word martyr, like jihad, is used more loosely in the Muslim world than in the West, notes Esposito: "Martyrdom, like jihad, has become a common term of praise for those who have died in struggles in Palestine (whether members of secular or Islamic groups), Iran, Egypt and Lebanon, as well as Azerbaijan, Bosnia, Chechnya, Kashmir and the southern Philippines."[13]

The Qur'an does promise martyrs *houris* (beautiful virgins) in heaven, but it does not say how many. Some scholars have said there will be two houris to a man, others say there will be seventy-two. But who or what, exactly, is a houri? Is she human or an extraterrestrial beauty? Moroccan feminist Fatima Mernissi says, "There are two paradises, one promised by the sacred text and the other representing the imam's male fantasies."[14]

Olivier Roy, the leading French authority on Islam, notes that suicide bombings are a relatively recent phenomenon among Muslims, started after the Israeli occupation of southern Lebanon. He asks, "Why should Muslims have discovered only in 1983 that suicide attacks are a good way to enter paradise?"[15] Another relevant question is this: if the sexual rewards of heaven are such a draw for men, what explains women suicide bombers?

Conclusion

There is no question that the concept of jihad has a great hold on Muslims, though not in the way most Westerners think. Jihad motivates Muslims, principally for peaceful individual purposes, to ward off temptations and to do good. But jihad can also be a collective rallying cry against oppression and occupation, as proven in Afghanistan against the Soviets and as seen among segments of Palestinians and, lately, Iraqis.

Given its central place in the Muslim universe, jihad has been invoked throughout Muslim history by the rulers and the ruled, the caliphs and the colonialists, as well as the rebels, in times of war and peace. Both the British and the French obtained *fatwas* (religious rulings) decreeing that since they were the legal rulers of their colonies, jihad against them was not permitted.

The 1967 Arab war against Israel was described as a jihad. So were Anwar Sadat's 1977 journey of peace to Jerusalem and the 1979 Camp David peace accord. So was his 1981 assassination (his killers rationalizing the murder as part of their jihad against Israel). So was Saddam Hussein's 1991 invasion of Kuwait. Now bin Laden invokes jihad for his terrorism.

Not everything bad that Muslims do can be attributed to Islam, any more than Christianity is to be blamed for some of the Christian Phalangists who participated in the massacre of Palestinians in the refugee camps of Beirut in 1982 with illustrations of the Virgin Mary on their gun butts (as did the Christian Serbs in Bosnia in the 1990s). As Huston Smith writes: "Jihad has been turned by outsiders into a rallying cry for hatred against Muslims."[16]

The final word here goes to Bishop Desmond Tutu. In a conversation with me in 2002, he said:

Christians would resent it very, very deeply if they were characterized by some of the weird fundamentalists in our camp. They would resent it very deeply if it is said that we are like the people in Northern Ireland who have been at each other's throats seemingly forever.

The Crusaders were Christians. Is that a justification for saying that Christianity is an aggressive religion?

Who was responsible for the Holocaust? Because some Christians did that, would we then say that Christianity is a violent religion?

Fascism — where did that come from? Europe.

Nazism? Europe.

Colonialism? Europe.

Does that justify our saying that all of that was due to Christianity?

Apartheid was supported by one of the major Christian churches in South Africa. Do you then say, "Ah, Christianity is responsible for all this racism?"

Hip-Hop

Islam is ingrained in the number one American cultural export — hip-hop. Ever since the emergence of this art form, Islamic references have served as a religious as well as a non-Western cultural identity for many African American singers.

> *I was raised like a Muslim*
> *Prayin to the East*
>   — Gang Starr, "Who's Gonna Take the Weight?" *Step in the Arena*

> *How dare you try to deny Allah's intelligence?*
>   — Wu-Tang Clan, "Jah World," *The W*

> *In the name of jesus, in the name of allah, in the spirit of the ancestors, amen.*
>   — Common, in CD booklet for *Be*

Rappers find parallels in the verses of the Qur'an and the rhyming pattern and structure of rap lyrics. Both the Qur'an and hip-hop use rhymed declarative prose that delivers powerful messages quickly. Mos Def, an African American convert, says, "The entire Qur'an rhymes. Like, you don't even notice it. *Bismillah/ al-Rahma/ nir-Rahim. Al-hamdu/ lillahi/ rab-bil/ aala meen.* It holds fast to your memory. And then you start to have a deeper relationship with it on recitation. You learn it and you recite it. Then one day you're reciting it, and you start to understand! You be like, 'Wow!'"[17]

Not all hip-hop artists are practicing Muslims, or belong to mainstream Islam, like Mos Def, Everlast or Freeway (who has done the Haj). It is difficult to tell which rappers are Muslim and which are not, given that many wear the *kufi*

(Muslim skullcap) for fashion rather than as a statement of faith. Some belong to Louis Farrakhan's Nation of Islam (Chuck D and Ice Cube) and others to the Nation's smaller offshoot, the Five Percent Nation (Busta Rhymes, Methodman, Rakim and Ghostface).[18]

Much of rap is un-Islamic or pseudo-Islamic — or just another sales gimmick. But overall, rap artists who call themselves Muslims credit Islam for turning their lives around.

Devout Islamic rappers — African American converts as well as the children of Muslim immigrants — include artists such as Kelly, Native Deen and Remarkable Current. Many perform only in drug-free and alcohol-free venues. Some have spoken out against both Muslim extremism and American wars on Muslim nations. Fredwreck, a Los Angeles-area rap producer, born Farid Nassar to Palestinian parents, urges fellow Muslims "to stand up and say, 'That extremist stuff ain't right.' There's nothing in the Qur'an that tells me to take it [violence] to innocent people."

Rappers in Egypt, Lebanon and the Israeli Occupied Territories, and in the Muslim minority communities of Germany, France, England and elsewhere in Europe are using the medium the way it was conceived — as protest poetry.

"The Turkish-German rap is a copycat of American rap but, being German, is less explicit and less violent," says Jana Simon, a German writer who specializes in intergenerational issues. She told me in 2005, "The Turkish kids here have developed their own dialect, a patois, and they are using it to communicate their alienation and the daily discrimination they encounter."

Chapter 6
The Future

Any attempt at mending the West's frayed relations with the Muslim world must begin with the recognition that just as the reasons given for the war on Iraq were proven to be false, most of the explanations tying terrorism to Islam have not stood the test of time.

When fifteen of the nineteen terrorists of 9/11 turned out to have been Saudi citizens, several experts blamed Wahhabism, the austere interpretation of Islam practiced in Saudi Arabia. The problem with the formulation was that the Saudi ruling family, the official guardians of Wahhabism, remains a staunch ally of the US and the chief guarantor of the energy needs of the West. Moreover, the Wahhabis have historically been more concerned with fellow Muslims, not non-Muslims.

We were told that terrorists were hatched primarily in Afghanistan, Pakistan and elsewhere in madrassahs, which were teaching extremism. But we know now that most of those who carried out the al Qaeda-like bombings in Bali, Jakarta, Istanbul, Amman and other places were not graduates of those schools but terrorists of disparate backgrounds, from the Middle East, Central and South Asia and the Far East. The bombers of the Madrid and London trains were young Muslims born or raised in Europe. So were the two Britons who went to Israel in 2003 to be suicide bombers. So were those who occasionally turned up in US-occupied Iraq to join the insurgency.

Another theory — crude, lewd, sensationalist and as obsessed with sex as the centuries-old Western fixation with the Prophet Muhammad's marriages — was that suicide bombers were inspired by Islam's promise of virgins in Paradise. That may have motivated the religiously inclined but not others, and certainly not women bombers such as the "black widows" of Chechnya, who had no such sexual favors to look forward to in heaven.

So we must return to earthly reasons for the terrorism involving Muslims. The wars and conflicts in Iraq and the Israeli Occupied Territories are not theological. Nor are those in Afghanistan, Kashmir and Chechnya. Equally, the domestic economic and political deprivations of hundreds of millions in the Muslim world have little to do with religion. The alienation of European Muslims is not a function of Islam but of European racism.

Muslims have worldly grievances galore, and it is these that need to be addressed. Otherwise, we may be at war forever.

Gijs de Vries, the European Union's counter-terrorism coordinator, has said, as plainly as possible, that American foreign policy is the major cause. A solution to the Arab-Israeli dispute won't eradicate terrorism, but it would eliminate one of the main tools of terrorist recruitment, he has said, adding that the same logic applies to Iraq.[1]

One of the biggest shortcomings of the war on terrorism was the complete misreading of Osama bin Laden's initial popularity among Muslims. He always had two constituencies — the few who joined his terrorist campaigns and the many who identified with his articulation of Muslim grievances. Western commentators analyzed his Islamic theology and ignored his political message. Muslim masses ignored his religious pronouncements but identified with his political grievances. But the West remains hobbled by its fixation with Islam. It needs to get over what French orientalist Maxime Rodinson famously called theologo-centrism — seeing Muslims solely or mostly through the prism of their religion.[2]

Like any other faith, Islam can be and is used by both fundamentalists and liberals, and by the violent and the peaceful, to rationalize their agendas. To blame terrorism on this or that holy book is to be intellectually lazy and politically dishonest. Besides, Muslims are no more going to rewrite the Qur'an than Jews are the Torah, Christians the Bible or Hindus the Mahabharata.

Laying collective guilt on Muslims may make good propaganda, but law-abiding Muslims are no more responsible for 9/11 and the London subway bombings and other heinous acts of terrorism than Japanese Canadians or Japanese Americans were for Pearl Harbor, or German Americans, German Canadians and German British were for Nazism. It is useful to recall what Anne Frank, hiding from the Nazis in Amsterdam during the Second World War, wrote in her famous diary: "When a Christian does something wrong, it's his fault. When a Jew does, it's the fault of all Jews."

Similarly, confusing religiosity with extremism is obtuse. Just because a Muslim is religious does not mean that he or she is a militant.

The West cannot tell Muslims which Islam to practice. The British, Italian and French colonialists tried that and failed. Conservative interpretations of Islam are as legitimate as conservative interpretations of Judaism and Christianity. It is fallacy to think that the only good Muslim is one who is secular, a minimalist believer, or not a believer at all. If anything, the West needs to be wary of those Muslims who may be too ready to parrot what it wants to hear. America lost Iran to the Islamic revolution in 1979 by listening mostly to pro-American Iranians. The Bush administration got into trouble in Iraq by accepting the tall tales told by exiled Iraqi politicians about weapons of mass destruction and how the invading American troops were going to be welcomed with flowers.

As long as the West keeps looking for anti-Islamic Muslims, it will fail. If it is waiting for Islam to be depoliticized, it will be waiting forever. As Swiss intellectual Tariq Ramadan says: "People have looked at Muslims and said, 'We thought they were going to put aside their religion.' But young Muslims in North America and Europe are replying, 'We're not ready to forget who we are, in order to become what you want us to be.'"[3] This is truer of Muslims living in Muslim lands.

The Bush administration needs to rethink its terminology, too. What does it mean, for example, by "political Islam," "extremist Islam," "Islamism" or "Islamist extremism"? Do these terms include Muslims who may not follow all the rituals of the religion but still have an Islamic consciousness and certainly a strong sense of solidarity with Muslims everywhere? The world needs better ways to distinguish between the many Muslims who want peaceful change and the few who advocate violence.

The war on terrorism has been a failure because it is widely seen as a war on Muslims, with the killing of tens of thousands of civilians in Iraq and Afghanistan, the oppression of Palestinians, the detention without charge of tens of thousands of Muslims in the West, the surveillance of millions and the hostile public discourse against Muslims and Islam. It was clear from the beginning that if the West were to make Islam a dirty word, Muslims would turn a deaf ear to the West. It has and they have. It is, therefore, not surprising that just as a historic Muslim reformation is underway, the West is not a party to it.

Muslim Reformation

One often hears that Muslims must come to terms with modernization. In several areas, they already have. Unlike, say, the Hutterites, Muslims have shown little religious resistance to technology. Unlike the Jehovah's Witnesses, Muslims do not oppose blood transfusions. Unlike some evangelical Christians, most Muslims do not object to stem cell research. Issues like birth control and abortion have been far less divisive in the Muslim world than in Western nations, especially the United States. In Malaysia, the national Council of Fatwa, which issues periodic religious rulings to guide Muslims, drew little or no criticism when it not only endorsed stem cell research but also organ transplants and artificial insemination between husband and wife.

Democracy is taking root among Muslims, and not just in Afghanistan and Iraq under American sponsorship. In fact, it has been making the steadiest progress where the United States is the least involved. More than half the world's Muslims live in varying degrees of freedom in developing democracies. Muslims in Indonesia, Malaysia, Bangladesh, India, Turkey and parts of Africa have rejected politicians and parties offering only empty Islamic slogans or promising the sharia. Muslim voters generally are opting for leaders and parties who, besides addressing the real bread-and-butter issues, can help them make sense of Islam in the contemporary world.

There is also a social and religious revolution underway. All the leading religious scholars — both in the Muslim world and among the Muslim minorities in the US, Canada and Europe — have rejected terrorism. Just a day before the July 2005 subway bombings in London, there was a conference in Jordan of 200 leading Muslim scholars, including representatives of Grand

Mufti Ali Jumaa of Egypt and Ayatollah Syed Ali Sistani, the most senior cleric in Iraq. They condemned not only terrorism but also the tendency of militant Muslims to brand moderate Muslims as infidels. In December 2005, more than fifty leaders of Muslim nations, meeting in Mecca, issued an unprecedented call to fight terrorism: "The Islamic nation is in a crisis. This crisis does not reflect on the present alone, but also on its future and the future of humanity at large. We need decisive action to fight deviant ideas because they are used to justify terrorism."[4] The Islamic Conference is known more for rhetoric and less for action; still, that acknowledgment was unprecedented.

Some of the reforms are being introduced from the top down, as in authoritarian Pakistan, Morocco and Saudi Arabia. But the biggest push is coming from grassroots movements, from Indonesia and Malaysia, through Turkey, Iran and the Middle East to the minority Muslim communities of the West. Rather than reflexively defending Muslim nations, many Muslims are beginning to speak out against the human rights violations across the Muslim world. Formal and informal debates are underway about the rights and wrongs of violence in the name of religion. Muslims are as revolted by terrorism as anybody else — more so, because it casts a long shadow over them all.

Muslims are coming to terms with Israel, in direct proportion to the easing of harsh Israeli treatment of Palestinians and the progress on peace. Besides Egypt, Jordan and Turkey, which have had close bilateral ties with Israel, other nations are moving toward opening up relations. It was significant that when President Pervez Musharraf spoke to a Jewish group in New York in August 2005, there were only muted protests back in Pakistan. It is the Israeli occupation of Palestinian land — not the Judaism of the Israelis — that angers Arabs, including Christian Arabs, and the larger Muslim world. Israel has every right to exist and prosper, but so do the Palestinians.

New Islamists in Egypt, Syria and elsewhere are challenging the orthodox clerical establishment and longstanding conservative interpretations of religious texts. In South, Southeast and Far East Asia there is a growing impatience with the semi-literate clerical class. Muslims in the West, benefiting from their democratic freedoms, are increasingly challenging orthodoxy and moving away from culture-specific religious practices.

The most credible reformist voices belong to those calling for changes on Islamic terms, rather than aping Western models. It is the pious who are making the most headway against militancy and terrorism. Women, not surprisingly, are leading the debate — not just on gender issues but on pluralism and other related matters.

Public discourse, too, is moderating. Despite the extremist rhetoric and anti-Semitic statements and cartoons, which are disproportionately publicized in the West, the tone of debate and discussion is changing significantly, even in places like Saudi Arabia, where the old Wahhabi intolerance of other Muslims is waning. Neighboring United Arab Emirates has approved a *jamat khana* (gathering place) for the Ismaili Muslim minority. These developments augur well for the much-needed opening of religious space for Christians, Jews, Hindus, Buddhists and others in Muslim societies that still resist pluralism.

More than ever in my lifetime I hear Muslims talk about the humanism of Islam, and its message of religious pluralism, as conveyed in the Qur'an:

There is no compulsion in religion (2:256).

To you your religion, and to me, mine (109:6).

*Whoever wills may believe, and whosoever wills
   may disbelieve* (18:29).

Had He willed, He would have guided you all (6:148).

*Had your Lord willed, everyone on Earth would have
   believed;
Do you then force everyone till they believed?* (10:99)

These injunctions ought to remind intolerant Muslims that if God had intended all mankind to be Muslims, He would have made them so. In fact, Allah elaborates on this elsewhere: *Most people, despite your keenness, won't become believers* (12:103).

Extremists are also being reminded that the wrath of God constitutes a minuscule part of the Qur'an. Of the ninety-nine names of Allah, ninety have to do with kindness, compassion, generosity and forgiveness. The believers are enjoined to pursue the moderate middle path, remembering that the first thing God commanded Muhammad to do was not go to war but to read: *Read in the name of the Lord who created you* (96:1). The most used word in the Qu'ran, after Allah, is *ilm* (knowledge).

An Era of Hope

The Muslim journey of reform is clearly underway. The West needs to get on with its own, by emancipating itself from its prejudices against and fear of Muslims and Islam, which severely hobble its relations with a third of humanity and undermine its own democratic ideals. Western democracies have had to battle anti-Catholicism and anti-Semitism, and still must in many ways. Their challenge in this age surely is to wrestle down Islamophobia.

Perhaps that, too, is underway. After all, millions of

Canadians, Americans, Britons, Italians, Spaniards and others marched against the unjust war on Iraq. Millions condemn the ongoing injustices against Muslims and are increasingly cognizant of the double standards employed against Muslims and Islam. More and more people are making unprecedented efforts at understanding Islam and reaching out to Muslims. An exponentially growing number of citizens are challenging the official narratives of war and rejecting the racist hypothesis about the inevitability of a clash of civilizations.

A congenitally optimistic Canadian I may be, but as a journalist tethered to reality, I can say with some confidence that we may, at last, be on the cusp of a new era of understanding.

Inshallah, God willing.

Notes

1 The Politics

1. The lower number, based on confirmed reports, is from Iraq Body Count, www.iraqbodycount.org, March 2006; the upper estimate is from Les Roberts et al., "Mortality Before and After the 2003 Invasion of Iraq: Cluster Sample Survey," *The Lancet* 364, Issue 9448, November 20, 2004, 1857-64.

2. UNICEF report on the effects of economic sanctions on Iraq, 1999.

3. *60 Minutes*, CBS, December 5, 1996.

4. *Time*, November 11, 2002.

5. *The World Factbook*, www.cia.gov/cia/publications/factbook/index. html; Statistics Canada, 2001 census.

6. Amnesty International, *Below the Radar: Secret Flights to Torture and "Disappearances,"* April 4, 2006.

7. Human Rights Watch. www.hrw.org.

8. Immigration Policy in Focus, *Targets of Suspicion: The Impact of Post-9/11 Policies on Muslims, Arabs and South Asians in the U.S.*, Vol. 3, Issue 2, May 2004.

9. Haroon Siddiqui, "Ayatollah Ashcroft's Law," *Toronto Star*, June 12, 2003.

10. James Yee, *For God and Country: Faith and Patriotism Under Fire* (New York: PublicAffairs, 2005).

11. www.news.cornell.edu/releases/Dec 04/Muslim.poll.bpf.htm/.

12. UN News Center, New York, "Confronting Islamophobia," December 7, 2004.

13. Tariq Ali, *Bush in Babylon: The Recolonization of Iraq* (London: Verso, 2003), 214.

14. International Helsinki Federation for Human Rights, www.ihf-hr.org/documents; Cornell University, www.news.cornell.edu/releases/Dec.04/muslim.poll.bpf.htm/; Associated Press, "Warning Issued On Rising Racism in Europe," September 14, 2004; BBC, "Anti-Muslim Bias Spreads in EU", March 7, 2005, www.news.bbc.co.uk/2/hi/Europe/4325225.stm; *The Times*, London, "Muslims Face Rising Suspicion in Europe," December 19, 2004; Claudia Deane and Darryl Frears, "Negative Perception of Islam Increasing," *Washington Post*, March 9, 2006.

15. Late Edition, CNN, July 13, 2003.

16. The sayings of the Prophet have been drawn mainly from three sources: Dr. Muhammad Muhsin Khan, trans./ed., *Sahih Al-Bukhari Summarized*, Arabic-English, (Riyadh, Saudi Arabia: Dar-us-Salam Books, 1994); Abdullah al-Suharwady, *Sayings of Muhammad* (Secaucus, New Jersey: Citadel Press, 1905, 1995); Thomas Cleary, trans. *The Wisdom of the Prophet: Sayings of Muhammad* (Boston: Shambhala, 2001).

17. Arab Human Development Report, United Nations, 2004

18. Quotations from the Qur'an are mostly from M.M. Pickthall, *The Qur'an Translated* (Washington, DC, ICSFP, 2005).

2 European Muslims

1. Josie Appleton, "Fundamentalism Begins at Home," Dec. 14, 2004, www.spiked-online.com/Articles/0000000CA816.htm

2. Frida Ghitis, "Europe Casts Wary Eye on France," *Toronto Star*, November 18, 2005.

3. "French Muslims Face Job Discrimination," "Muslims in Europe," www.bbc.co.uk

4. "Elite French Schools Block the Poor's Path to Power," *New York Times*, December 18, 2005.

5. Kofi Annan, "Why Europe Needs an Immigration Strategy," from a speech made to the European Parliament, January 29, 2004,

www.un.org/news/ossg/sg/stories/sg-29jan2004.htm; "Aging
Europe Finds Its Pension Is Running Out," *New York Times*, June
29, 2003.

6. Jytte Klausen, *The Islamic Challenge: Politics and Religion in Western
Europe* (Oxford: Oxford University Press, 2005).

7. US Department of State, Washington, DC, "French Muslims Favor
Integration," May 24, 2005.

8. Barnard Godard, *Formation des Imams*, quoted by Jytte Klausen in
The Islamic Challenge, 116.

9. 10 billion Euros in general taxpayer funding and 8.5 billion in
"church tax" collected by the government on behalf of the two
churches.

10. Interview with *Le Figaro*, August, 2004.

11. *Le Monde*, May 17, 2005.

12. Tariq Ramadan, *To Be a European Muslim* (Leicester: Islamic
Foundation, 1999); *Islam, the West and the Challenges of Modernity*
(Leicester: Islamic Foundation, 2001).

13. Gary Younge, "The Right to be Offended," *The Nation*, February
27, 2006.

14. *New York Times*, "Cartoon Dispute Prompts Identity Crisis for
Liberal Denmark," February 12, 2006.

15. Reuters, "Denmark Accuses Imams of Whipping Up Cartoon
Row," February 8, 2006.

16. *New York Times*, "Denmark Is Unlikely Front in Islam-West
Culture Wars," January 8, 2006.

17. In an interview with the author, 2005.

18. Guy Coq, "Scarves and Symbols," *New York Times*, January 30,
2004.

3 The Faith

1. Ziauddin Sardar and Zafar Abbas Malik, *Muhammad for Beginners*
(Cambridge: Icon, 1994), 28.

2. Hammid Abbas, *Story of the Great Expansion* (Jeddah: Al Bilal Printing, 1996), 175, 214-15, 365, 372; *Aramco Magazine* (Houston: Saudi Aramco Oil Co., May/June 2002).

3. "For Muslims, Loans for the Conscience," *New York Times*, August 7, 2005.

4. *Newsweek*, "Money Talks, Major Western Banks Coming to Dominate Booming Global Market in Islamic Finance," August 8, 2005.

5. Huston Smith, *Islam: A Concise Introduction* (San Francisco: Harper, 2001), 76.

6. Malise Ruthven, *Islam in the World* (Oxford: Oxford University Press, 1984 and 2000), 240.

4 Women

1. Guity Nashat, in "Introduction", *Women in Islam: From Medieval to Modern Times* by Wiebke Walther (Princeton: Markus Wiener Publications, 1995), 7-8.

2. Reza Aslan, *No God but God* (New York: Random House, 2005), 72-73.

3. 2005 report of the Women's Empowerment and Development Organization, an American NGO charting women's progress since the 1995 United Nations-sponsored conference on women in Beijing.

4. www.ithaca.edu/faculty/abarlas.

5. Jamal Badawi, *Gender Equity in Islam* (Plainfield, Indiana: American Trust Publications, 1995), 4.

6. web.amnesty.org/actforwomen/domestic-index-eng.

7. *New York Times*, "Sweden Boldly Exposes a Secret Side of Women's Lives," April 6, 2005.

8. Sharon LaFraniere, "Entrenched Epidemic: Wife Beatings – Africa," *New York Times*, August 11, 2005.

9. Chris McGreal, "Murdered in the Name of Honor," *Guardian*

Weekly, July 1-7, 2005.

10. Camille Bains, "Indo-Canadians Caught in a Clash of Cultures," *Toronto Star*, June 25, 2005.

11. Sebnem Arsu, "Turks to Fight 'Honor Killing' of Women," *New York Times*, May 16, 2005.

12. "Islam United to Stop Genital Mutilation," *The Rabat Declaration*, November, 2005.

13. Wiebke Walther, *Women in Islam*, 57.

14. Genevieve Oger, *Deutsche Welle*, July 31, 2005 (posted on the website of Women Living Under Muslim Laws).

15. Fatima Mernissi, *The Veil and the Male Elite: A Feminist Interpretation of Women's Rights in Islam* (Reading, Massachusetts: Addison-Wesley, 1987), 104-105.

16. Martin Lings, *Muhammad: His Life Based on the Earliest Sources* (Rochester, Vermont: Inner Traditions International, 1983), 35.

17. A.A. Engineer, *The Qur'an, Women and Modern Society* (Kuala Lumpur: Synergy Books International, n.d.), 23.

18. Aisha Bewley, *Islam: The Empowering of Women* (London: Ta-Ha Publishers, 1999), 31.

19. Guity Nashat, "Introduction", *Women in Islam*, 6-7.

20. Philip K. Hitti, *The History of the Arabs*, 6th ed. (New York: St. Martin's, 1958), 333. First published in 1937 by Macmillan.

21. Waleed Aly, "A Smarter Way to Fight for Muslim Women," *The Age*, March 9, 2005.

22. www.ithaca.edu/faculty/abarlas.

23. Malise Ruthven, *Fundamentalism: The Search for Meaning* (Oxford: Oxford University Press, 2004), 115.

24. Zainah Anwar, "The Experience of Sisters in Islam," paper presented at a conference of the International Human Rights Law Group, October 10, 2003 (posted on the website of Women Living Under Muslim Laws).

25. Fatima Mernissi, *The Veil and the Male Elite*, 24.

26. Laurie Goldstein, "Muslim Women Seeking a Place," *New York Times*, July 22, 2004.

27. Margot Badran, "Islamic Feminism: What's in a Name?" *Al-Ahram Weekly*, January 17-23, 2002.

28. Riffat Hassan, "Are Human Rights Compatible with Islam?", www.religionsconsultation.org/hassan2.htm.

5 Jihad and Terrorism

1. John Esposito, *What Everyone Needs to Know About Islam* (Oxford: Oxford University Press, 2002), 119.

2. Rudolph Peters, *Jihad in Classical and Modern Islam* (Princeton: Markus Wiener Publishers, 1996), 1.

3. Mahmud Shaltut's essay in Arabic has been translated by Rudolph Peters and included in his book *Jihad in Classical and Modern Islam*, 97, 113.

4. *Ibid.*, 82.

5. *Ibid.*, 77.

6. Huston Smith, *Islam: A Concise Introduction* (San Francisco: Harper, 2001), 72.

7. Associated Press, "Islamic Nations Vow to Combat Extremist Ideology," December 12, 2005.

8. John Esposito, *What Everyone Needs to Know About Islam*, 119.

9. Philip Gourevitch, "Letter from Sri Lanka: Tides of War," *New Yorker*, August 1, 2005.

10. Robert Pape, *Dying to Win: The Strategic Logic of Suicide Terrorism* (New York: Random House, 2005).

11. Robert Pape, interview with *The American Conservative*, July 18, 2005.

12. Huston Smith, *Islam*, ix, x.

13. John Esposito, *What Everyone Needs to Know*, 134.

14. Fatima Mernissi, *Women in Moslem Paradise* (New Delhi: Kali for Women, 1986), 23.

15. Josie Appleton, "Fundamentalism Begins at Home," Dec. 14, 2004, www.spiked-online.com/Articles/0000000CA816.htm

16. Huston Smith, *Islam*. ix.

17. Hesham Samy Abdel-Alim, "Hip-Hop Islam," *Al-Ahram*, July 7-13, 2005.

18. The name Five Percent emanates from their belief that only 5 percent of the population has true knowledge, while 10 percent have some but use it to rule over the remaining 85 percent.

6 The Future

1. BBC News, "Marginalized Muslims Cause Concern," March 11, 2005. www.bbc.co.uk/world/Europe.

2. Maxime Rodinson, *Europe and the Mystique of Islam* (London: I.B. Tauris, 1988).

3. Tariq Ramadan, "Muslims: To Thine Own Self Be True," *Globe and Mail*, October 13, 2005.

4. Associated Press, "Islamic Nations Vow to Combat Extremist Ideology," December 12, 2005.

Essential Reading

Dozens of articles, books and websites were consulted for this book. Many are listed in the notes on pages 149 to 155. But I do recommend the following titles:

Armstrong, Karen. *Islam: A Short History.* New York: Modern Library, 2002.

Aslan, Reza. *No God but God.* New York: Random House, 2005.

Barks, Coleman, Trans. *The Essential Rumi.* San Francisco: HarperCollins, 1995.

Ebadi, Shirin. *Iran Awakening.* New York: Random House, 2006.

El Fadl, Khaled Abou. *Islam and the Challenge of Democracy,* Princeton: Princeton University Press, 2004.

Esposito, John. *What Everyone Needs to Know About Islam.* Oxford: Oxford University Press, 2002.

Lings, Martin. *Muhammad: His Life Based on the Earliest Sources.* Rochester, Vermont: Inner Traditions International Ltd., 1983.

Mamdani, Mahmood, *Good Muslim, Bad Muslim.* New York: Pantheon, 2003.

Pickthall, M. M. *Muhammad: A Brief History.* Beltsville: Amana Publications, 1998.

Pickthall, M.M. *The Quran Translated.* Washington, D.C., IC.SFP, 2005.

Sardar, Ziauddin and Zafar Abbas Malik, *Muhammad for Beginners,* Cambridge: Icon Books, 1994.

Smith, Huston. *Islam: A Concise Introduction.* San Francisco, Harper, 2001.

Index